DEFENDING THE EARTH

DEFENDING THE EARTH

Debate between Murray Bookchin and Dave Foreman

Foreword by David Levine

Montreal/New York

BLACK ROSE BOOKS No. U162
Paperback ISBN: 0-921689-88-8
Hardcover ISBN: 0-921689-89-6

Canadian Cataloguing in Publication Data

Bookchin, Murray, 1921 -
  Defending the Earth

Canadian ed.
ISBN 0-921689-89-6 (bound)—
  ISBN 0-921689-88-8 (pbk.)

1. Human ecology — United States.
2. Environmental policy — United States —Citizen participation. I. Foreman, Dave, 1946- II. Title

JA75.8.B66.   1991   363.7'0524   C91-090084-1

Cover Design: Associés Libres

Editorial Offices
BLACK ROSE BOOKS
3981 St-Laurent Boulevard,
Suite 444
Montréal, Québec
H2W 1Y5 Canada

BLACK ROSE BOOKS
340 Nagel Drive
Cheektowaga, New York
14225 USA

Mailing Address
BLACK ROSE BOOKS
P.O. Box 1258
Succ. Place du Parc
Montréal, Québec H2W 2R3
Canada

Table of Contents

Turning Debate Into Dialogue

David Levine

Founder and Director, The Learning Alliance

This small but important book grows out of "The Great Debate." That's what—for months in advance—many environmental activists around the country called the first public meeting between social ecology theorist Murray Bookchin and deep ecology activist Dave Foreman. Most expected political fireworks at the joint talk organized in November 1989 by the Learning Alliance, New York City's alternative education and action organization.

Given the confrontational rhetoric and the all-too-frequent name-calling that has characterized the volatile political debate between various advocates of "social ecology" and "deep ecology," the expectation of sparks flying was quite understandable. Over the last few years, the radical ecology movement has been torn by bitter ideological divisions. One of the most serious divisions, and certainly the one which has received the most play in the media, has been between "deep" and "social" ecology—between a "biocentric" philosophy which makes protecting the welfare of the wilderness the most essential human project and a left-libertarian "ecological humanist" philosophy which sees radical social transformation as the main key to defending the Earth.

In recognition of the seriousness of this ongoing and often heated debate, the Learning Alliance set up a face-to-face meeting between Bookchin, a founder of the Institute of Social Ecology and an influential philosopher within the international green movement, and Foreman,

1

a founder of, and, at the time, an important spokesperson for Earth First!. Both Bookchin and Foreman had been among the most vocal contenders in the debate between deep and social ecology philosophies over the last few years.

The Learning Alliance, however, never intended this event to be a "debate" in any conventional sense. It was meant, instead, to be a constructive dialogue between two articulate spokespeople from different wings of the relatively small, but potentially powerful, radical ecology movement. We sought a dialogue that identified common ground and complementary differences, as well as one that carefully probed areas of serious disagreement. We were looking for a renewed sense of unity-in-diversity and a higher level of political discussion within the movement.

At the Learning Alliance, we are convinced that the radical ecology movement cannot afford to expend its time and energy in unproductive and divisive infighting, particularly in light of the continuing harassment of the movement by the Federal Bureau of Investigation. While we agree that important differences in philosophy, analysis, vision, and strategy should be vigorously addressed, we feel this is best done in respectful and cooperative situations whenever and wherever possible. While a few of our differences may actually be contradictory, many others are complementary and can actually strengthen our movement if recognized and appreciated. Furthermore, at least some of our differences can be resolved rather than endlessly argued. Our goal for this event was to create a cooperative forum for just such ground-breaking discussions.

Thanks to the generous spirit evidenced by both Bookchin and Foreman, the event was a success. Bookchin, who spoke first, set the tone of reconciliation and mutual respect by declaring that he stands "shoulder to shoulder with everyone in Earth First! who is trying to save the wilderness." Foreman replied by acknowledging that the greed of multinational corporations and the power of competitive nation-states threatens human dignity and social justice as well as the evolutionary integrity of the natural world. Echoing Bookchin, he asserted that our various movements, whatever their primary emphases, need to address, or at least respect, both the struggle for the well-being of humanity and the struggle for the survival and well-being of all other species. "We face the same enemy no matter what we emphasize," argued Foreman.

Indeed, both Bookchin and Foreman agreed that as long as hierarchical social relationships are the foundation for our societies, there is very little hope for creating an ecological society that will not seek to dominate or exploit the Earth. Similarly, both agreed that protecting wilderness areas and fostering a new ecological sensibility and a direct moral concern for other species was an urgent task that could no longer be ignored or postponed.

This fragile but real unity between Bookchin and Foreman and their clearly stated respect for diversity within the movement represent an important achievement. Such principled unity is important because thousands of people are now becoming active in seeking a sustainable and ecologically sound future—whether by organizing against toxic wastes, setting up recycling centers, purchasing "green products," participating in Earth Day events, contributing to environmental organizations, or protesting corporate environmental degradation. While these initial efforts often fall short of the level of understanding and activism that is necessary, they do represent an important step forward. They are a foundation upon which a broad-based, radical ecology movement can ultimately be built.

To achieve this goal, however, today's radical ecologists need to focus their strongest criticisms not against each other, but against those institutional forces which are the source of so much of today's environmental degradation and which are now trying to co-opt and contain the growing grassroots reform movement that is emerging in this country and throughout the world. While there is certainly room for diverse philosophical and strategic approaches within an effective movement to defend the Earth, there is certainly no room within our movement for major timber companies who claim that "Every day is Earth Day" while they continue to clearcut major sections of the Northwest. There is no room for chemical companies who are producing hazardous materials and, at the same time, claim that they are producing environmentally safe products now that they are repackaging them in a green bottle. There is no room for the many other corporate and political interests who claim their exploitative policies are healthy for either the Earth or its people. The ecology movement needs to mean more than that.

The negative effects of these corporate and government "environmentalists" are already being felt. A number of big environmental organizations have corporate and politically conservative voices among their executive staff, their boards, and their funders. The result, of course, is more and more compromised positions, more and more timid strategies, and, ultimately, a more and more ineffective ecology movement. The examples are, unfortunately, all too plentiful: from "mainstream" environmental organizations which allow destructive development projects to move forward at the request of business forces within their organization to groups which advocate "responsible" legislation to protect one or two endangered species while they allow the rain forests and lifeways of indigenous people to be economically plundered and drastically altered without protest.

Fortunately, as the discussion between Murray Bookchin and Dave Foreman shows, a potential counterforce to this corporate "environmentalism" has been growing for some time. Indeed, there is a diverse proliferation of more radical ecological schools of thought and action including deep ecologists, social ecologists, eco-feminists, bioregionalists, Native American traditionalists, eco-socialists, and greens. These small groups have the potential to reach out to the general public and the growing grassroots environmental movement in educational and empowering ways that can transform today's reformist environmental movement into a broad-based movement seeking fundamental change. I believe that the future of the planet may well depend on how effectively today's radical ecologists can work together and build such a movement.

It would be a crime, I think, if today's pioneering radical ecologists allowed principled political debate and dialogue among themselves to degenerate into sectarian squabbles and ego-bashing. Successful social movements are not built this way. If radical ecologists continue to approach their differences in such destructive, combative ways, they will likely only end up alienating rather than educating the expanding segment of the general public that is beginning to face up to the reality of the ecological crisis. Luckily, as the dialogue between Bookchin and Foreman recreated and expanded in this book so clearly attests, building a principled unity-in-diversity is possible.

In Chapter 1, as in the original dialogue, Bookchin and Foreman begin to cooperatively explore their differing, but often overlapping, perspectives on a wide range of issues: nature philosophy, environmental ethics, social theory, and social change strategy. In Chapter 2, prompted by comments and questions from Paul McIsaac, a longtime activist and a reporter for National Public Radio, both Foreman and Bookchin discuss their views on what the radical left tradition offers or doesn't offer to the radical ecology movement. In Chapter 3, Linda Davidoff, executive director of New York City's Park Council, challenges both Bookchin and Foreman on their negative views of reformist social change strategies and sparks each of them to spell out how they each think their more radical visions and strategies can be realistic and effective in the less-than-perfect political world here and now. In Chapter 4, Jim Haughton, a leader of the black community group Harlem Fight Back, sparks an important discussion between Foreman and Bookchin by raising the particularly thorny issue of racism in the ecology movement and how this affects the future of the planet.

The result of these discussions is a surprising amount of agreement even though some important differences still exist (some of which are taken up in Chapters 5 and 6 of this book which were written especially for this book by Foreman and Bookchin a year after the original dialogue took place). These differences, along with several others, need to be explored even further and, if possible, resolved. To its credit, this book points the way forward. Besides being packed with provocative ideas and insights, this book is a model of how best to raise difficult political differences within a movement. If Bookchin and Foreman can do it, then so can the rest of us.

This book proves that there are creative opportunities within the radical ecology movement for building alliances and connections across community, issue, race, gender, class, and political lines. If nature itself shows the need for diverse species to co-exist within any particular environment, then we humans should also understand the imperative of unity through diversity. The struggle across this country and the world for more meaningful communities, institutions, and ways of life is not an easy task. It will require the cooperation of those who choose to stop bulldozers in wilderness areas, who work to counter racism within the urban ecology of our cities, who develop alternative technologies, who directly challenge major environmental plunderers, who try to revive and strengthen the empowering institutions and processes of grassroots democracy, and who encourage a deeper spiritual understanding of the natural world and the human community.

Not surprisingly, this book itself represents the cooperative work of several people. My thanks, of course, go out especially to Murray Bookchin and Dave Foreman. Thanks also go to Paul McIsaac, Linda Davidoff, and Jim Haughton who added so much to the discussion and to South End Press for making this important and historic dialogue available in book form. I particularly want to thank Greg Bates from South End, who came up with the orignal idea for publishing this dialogue as a book, and Steve Chase, the South End editor who was able to "translate" and expand a taped conversation into an accessible, readable book as well as write an insightful introduction to this dialogue. Several people read and commented on various parts of this manuscript. These people include Janet Biehl, John Davis, Bill Lynn, Patrick McNamara, Roxanne Pacheco, Kirkpatrick Sale, and Bill Weinburg. The Learning Alliance is proud to have been a partner in this important project.

Whither the Radical Ecology Movement?

Steve Chase

Since at least as far back as 1866, when the German biologist Ernest Haeckel coined the term "ecology," scientific ecologists have repeatedly split into different camps in how they view the question of humanity's proper place and role within nature. According to historian Donald Worster, "one might very well cast the history of ecology as a struggle between rival views of the relationship between humans and nature: one view devoted to the discovery of intrinsic value and its preservation, the other to the creation of an instrumentalized world and its exploitation."[1]

It should come as no surprise then that this same philosophical conflict splits the ranks of today's political activists who seek to reshape our society's relations with the rest of the natural world along more ecological lines. In his recent book, *Green Political Thought*, English author Andrew Dobson draws an important distinction between "light green" reform environmentalism and "dark green" radical ecologism. According to Dobson, conventional environmentalism represents an instrumental, imperial approach to nature that argues that our environmental problems, however serious, "can be solved without fundamental changes in present values or patterns of production and consumption." Radical ecologism, in contrast, raises the ethical ideal of a beloved eco-community and "argues that care for the environment...presupposes radical changes in our relationship with it, and in our mode of social and political life."[2]

This difference in political orientation, while perhaps not yet obvious to the general public, is not news to most people who are actively concerned with ecological politics today. The distinction between reform environmentalism and radical political ecologism was first made over 25 years ago. This book's co-author, Murray Bookchin, was among the first to draw attention to this distinction in several pioneering essays during the 1960s and 1970s. As Bookchin has noted, ecologism "refers to a broad, philosophical, almost spiritual, outlook toward humanity's relationship to the natural world, not to environmentalism [which is] a form of natural engineering that seeks to manipulate nature as mere 'natural resources' with minimal pollution and public outcry."[3]

In strikingly similar terms, the renowned Norwegian eco-philosopher and activist Arne Naess made the same basic distinction in a 1973 essay contrasting the "shallow" reform environmental movement with the emerging "deep, long-range ecology movement."[4] While this essay did not receive significant attention in the U.S. until 1980, it is now quite common in both activist and academic circles to characterize the central political fault line within the ecology movement as the ideological division between "shallow" and "deep" ecologists. For many, "deep ecology" has become a generic rubric to describe all political ecologists who a) believe that the natural world has an intrinsic value of its own, b) seek to end industrial society's attempted domination of the biosphere, and c) work to radically reconstruct human society along ecological lines. In this very broad sense, social ecologists, eco-feminists, bioregionalists, radical greens, Earth First!ers, Native American traditionalists, many academic eco-philosophers, and some animal liberationists can all fairly be called "deep ecologists."

It thus came as a surprise to many ecology activists when Murray Bookchin strongly challenged the political perspective of deep ecology in the summer of 1987 at the second National Green Gathering at Amherst, Massachusetts. In his keynote address to the conference, Bookchin warned that the academic philosophers of deep ecology as well as several leading spokespeople for Earth First!, the self-proclaimed "action wing of deep ecology movement," were guilty of propagating a deeply flawed and potentially dangerous ecological perspective. In that speech, and in several later articles, Bookchin declared that the growing popularity of deep ecology suggests that a "major crisis of purpose, conscience, and direction exists in the U.S. ecology movement."[5]

Was Bookchin rejecting his long standing commitment to radical ecologism? Accustomed to the generic usage of the term deep ecology to describe the whole radical wing of the ecology movement, many activists interpreted the ensuing social vs. deep ecology debate as the latest volley between shallow environmentalism (admittedly combined this time with a radical social politics) and a deeper, more radical ecological philosophy, analysis, vision, and strategy. This interpretation, however, ignores the important shift in the meaning of the term deep ecology that occurred between the time Naess first used the term in 1973 and when Bookchin finally challenged the deep ecology perspective.

By the mid-1980s, the term deep ecology had increasingly come to mean Deep Ecology—a very particular, though eclectic, body of ideas developed by academics such as Naess, Warwick Fox, George Sessions, and Bill Devall on the one hand and by militant wilderness activists in Earth First! such as Ed Abbey, Christopher Manes, and Dave Foreman on the other. As Warwick Fox notes, "The term *deep ecology* can therefore be seen as one that does double duty, referring on the one hand to a whole class of approaches (i.e., all nonanthropocentric approaches) and on the other hand to a particular kind of approach within this class...a distinctive kind of approach to nonanthropocentrism."[6] This distinctive approach is the deep ecology perspective criticized so strenuously by Bookchin.

The deep vs. social ecology debate is thus not a heated rehash of the old environmentalism/ecologism debate. It is best understood as an intense dialogue across a new philosophical and political fault line that has emerged from within radical ecologism itself. At its heart, the debate between social and deep ecology suggests the existence of differing answers to the question, "Whither the radical ecology movement?"

Yet, even among those activists who recognize the novel nature of the debate, many were still surprised at the sharpness of Bookchin's critique of deep ecology. Were social and deep ecology really so far apart? Bookchin himself had long advocated, indeed pioneered, several of the key insights championed by deep ecologists. According to

Roderick Nash, a historian of American environmental ethics, Bookchin's theoretical work in social ecology, which began in the early 1950s, contributed greatly to the development of deep ecology in the 1970s and 1980s.[7] Indeed, one of Bookchin's essays on nature philosophy was included in the first anthology on deep ecology published in the United States, and he was prominently quoted as a deep ecology pioneer in the popular *Deep Ecology* manifesto written by George Sessions and Bill Devall a year later in 1985.[8] As Christopher Manes has noted, "up until [the U.S. green gathering in] 1987, Bookchin's works often received high praise in Deep Ecology literature."[9]

Few activists familiar with the literature on radical ecological philosophy would disagree that there are some significant differences in the philosophical origins, strategic focuses, and primary concerns of social and deep ecology. Yet most—at least up until the Green Gathering in Amherst—felt that these differences were not a significant problem. Unity-in-diversity is a basic attribute of healthy eco-communities. Why shouldn't it be a healthy characteristic for the radical ecology movement?

In his Amherst speech, Bookchin posed the question of whether these differences were, or could become, complementary or whether the two schools of thought were fundamentally, and inevitably, antagonistic. After reflecting on the work of several academic deep ecologists and on the published statements of a few Earth First! activists, Bookchin decided that deep and social ecology were fundamentally antagonistic after all. His assessment, put in its simplest terms, was that deep ecology was not just a radical pro-nature philosophy, but that it was potentially—and, in some cases, explicitly—anti-social and anti-human.

Bookchin's critique was soon answered by several people in the deep ecology movement and the resulting debate, as well as back and forth charges of "misanthropy" and "anthropocentrism," quickly spilled over into the pages of *Earth First!*, *The Nation*, *Utne Reader*, *Z Magazine*, *The Guardian*, *Socialist Review*, *Environmental Ethics*, *Mother Jones*, *Green Perspectives*, *Our Generation*, *Whole Earth Review*, *Green Letter*, *Omni*, *The New York Times* and popular books like Christopher Manes' *Green Rage*. Over the last few years, the debate has increasingly become a lively topic of discussion in movement circles. Perhaps never before has there been such a widespread political debate in the United States on the interrelationship between environmental ethics, nature philosophy, and radical social theory.

Unfortunately, until the face-to-face meeting between Dave Foreman and Murray Bookchin that provides the core of this book, the debate frequently tended to generate more heat than light. A number of grassroots ecology activists have been dismayed by the hostile, almost sectarian, nature of the debate. Some blame Bookchin and the social ecologists who have admittedly offered fierce and sweeping criticisms. Bookchin, for instance, characterized some of the leading lights of Earth First! as "barely disguised racists, survivalists, macho Daniel Boones, and outright social reactionaries." Foreman was perhaps the most frequent target of Bookchin's wrath. In his speech at Amherst, Bookchin called Foreman "a patently anti-humanist and macho mountain man" guilty of "a crude eco-brutalism."[10]

Others blame deep ecologists for the rancorous, all-or-nothing, tone of the debate. While Dave Foreman largely avoided critical outbursts and name-calling, naturalist writer Ed Abbey, the literary inspiration of Earth First!, publicly called Bookchin a "fat old lady" and declared that he didn't care if that "sounded sexist."[11] In a somewhat more civil response, Bill Devall publicly reversed his earlier opinion of Bookchin's work and started characterizing social ecology as just another "old paradigm" leftist ideology that falls far short of a genuinely ecological philosophy.[12] Christopher Manes went so far as to charge Bookchin with a "Faustian ambition to seize control of evolution" and dominate nature.[13]

Several rank and file activists responded to the intense and often angry tone of this debate with a "plague-on-both-your-houses" weariness and treated it as little more than an intellectual "cock-fight" without serious political substance. Yet most activists realize that, regardless of the relative merit of the rhetorical fireworks, some very real and important issues are at stake here, issues that need to be explored and resolved one way or another if the radical ecology movement is going to play a creative and influential role within our society in the years ahead.

Back in 1982, Roderick Nash observed that two different visions have emerged within the radical ecology movement over the last two or three decades. Nash calls these different radical ecological scenarios the "wilderness" vision and the "garden" vision.[14] If he were to write about these differing visions today, he might well connect these different visionary alternatives to deep ecology and social ecology. While these different visions are not necessarily mutually exclusive, they have, up to now, rarely been well integrated and they have frequently been formulated in extreme, near exclusive ways. This extremism may well be the primary source of conflict between proponents of deep and social ecology.

Nash, for example, believes that deep ecology wilderness lovers have much to fear from the advocates of the garden vision. As he puts it,

> There are two ways of thinking about the end of wilderness on earth. One might be termed the *wasteland scenario*. It anticipates a ravaged planet; one which is paved and poisoned to the point that the world dies with T.S. Eliot's celebrated whimper. This nightmare of creeping urbanization traditionally fired the protests of nature lovers, conservationists, and preservationists. It could still occur, especially given the increase of technological capability, but the greatest long-term threat to the interests of people who covet the wild may reside in the *garden scenario*. It too ends wilderness, but beneficently rather than destructively. René Dubos points the way with his vision of a bounteous, stable and, to many tastes, beautiful earth that is totally modified. In a garden-earth the fertility of the soil is not only maintained but enhanced. Fruit trees support songbirds. Carefully managed streams run clear and pure. The air is unpolluted. Forests provide an endless supply of wood. Large cities are rare as people decentralize into the hinterland. Many live on self-sufficient family farms. The animals permitted to exist are safe and useful. A softer variety of technology enables [people] to live gracefully and gratefully as part of the natural community. There is a minimum of pavement, cows dot the meadows, democracy thrives, and the kids have [healthy faces.] It is an appealing vision whose roots run back through Thomas Jefferson's deification of the yeoman farmer to the Garden of Eden.[15]

At first glance, at least, the garden scenario described by Nash bears more than a passing resemblance to the utopian vision of social ecology. Murray Bookchin, after all, described microbiologist René Dubos in 1974 as an important early social ecology thinker.[16] While Bookchin's and Dubos' views were far from identical even then, their visions for the *humanly inhabited* portions of the Earth did overlap significantly. Bookchin, however, expressed himself in much more radical terms. Following Peter Kropotkin, the visionary nineteenth-century anarchist geographer, Bookchin has argued that we need to transform our oppressive industrial capitalist society into "an ecological society based on non-hierarchical relationships, decentralized democratic communities, and eco-technologies like solar power, organic agriculture, and humanly scaled industries."[17]

According to Bookchin, decentralized forms of production and food cultivation tailored to the carrying capacities of particular bioregions are not only more efficient and ecologically sustainable, they also restore humanity's intimate contact with soil, plant and animal life, sun, and wind. This, he believes, is the only way to fully anchor and sustain a widespread ecological sensibility within our culture. Furthermore, he maintains that only by challenging the profit-seeking, "grow or die" dynamic of the corporate capitalist economy and creating an alternative economy oriented to ecologically sustainable production to meet vital human needs can we genuinely protect the planet from the ravages of acid rain, global warming, and ozone destruction.

Bookchin, of course, is not the only modern radical ecological thinker to draw on Kropotkin. Several writers, including some deep ecologists, have echoed Kropotkin's eco-anarchist ideas of communitarian democracy, deurbanization, industrial decentralization, alternative technology, organic agriculture, limits to growth, and a renewed naturalist sensibility. Social ecology, however, is the body of ideas that has most self-consciously built on this eco-anarchist foundation and further developed and elaborated a workable vision of "an ecological society." In doing so, social ecology makes an enormous contribution to the radical ecology movement, one which is neglected at our peril. Earth First! activist Judi Bari is sadly ill-informed when she maintains that the contours of an ecological society are "not spoken to in any leftist theory."[18]

Important questions remain, however: What do social ecologists have to say about the remaining wilderness areas of the planet that are increasingly encroached on and destroyed by our expansionary industrial society? Will wilderness be valued and allowed to flourish in the social ecology vision of the future? Are social ecologists fully sensitive to the call of environmental ethics beyond the moral imperative to provide a sustainable, healthy, beautiful, and productive natural environment for all members of the *human* community?

If we take Dubos as the definitive social ecologist, the answer is clearly no. Towards the end of his life, Dubos adopted a very exclusive and totalistic version of the garden vision and advocated "humanizing" and "managing" the entire surface of the planet. His vision, as Nash points out, was of a planet "totally modified," albeit prudently and carefully, by human intervention. Dubos was, in fact, quite open about the consequences of his perspective. As he put it, "the humanization of Earth inevitably results in destruction of wilderness and of many living species that depend on it."[19] This is seen by Dubos as an acceptable price to pay as we move the planet toward a new stage of humanly-managed natural evolution. Deep ecologists are quite right to criticize this extremist version of the garden vision. It does represent a form of anthropocentric, albeit sustainable, hubris.

In sharp contrast, however, Murray Bookchin has never embraced such a one-sided garden vision. While some of Bookchin's deep ecology critics have repeatedly tried to paint Bookchin's views as if they were identical to those of Dubos, such charges are very wide of the mark.[20] In his most important philosophical work, *The Ecology of Freedom,* Bookchin adamantly rejects the vision of a completely "domesticated" and "pacified" planet, calling instead for an appreciation of "a high degree of natural spontaneity" and urging "caution in disturbing natural processes."[21] Furthermore, since as far back as the 1960s, Bookchin has repeatedly asserted that one of the essential goals of social ecology is to "guard and *expand* wilderness areas and domains for wildlife."[22]

Significantly, Bookchin bases his views on ethical as well as practical grounds. Unlike reform environmentalism, says Bookchin, social ecology "sees the balance and integrity of the biosphere as an end in itself."[23] "Natural diversity," he says, "is to be cultivated not only because the more diversified the components that make up an ecosystem, the more stable the ecosystem; diversity is also desirable for its own sake, a value to be cherished as part of a spiritized notion of the living universe."[24] Other social ecologists, such as John Clark, have echoed Bookchin's nonanthropocentric approach to environmental ethics and argued the need for "humanity to situate its good within the larger context of the planetary good."[25]

Bookchin's and Clark's views on wilderness and environmental ethics are very different from Dubos'. Philosopher Thomas Berry has argued that it is best to call Dubos' approach "humanist ecology" and to clearly distinguish it from social ecology.[26] Bookchin would no doubt agree. He has certainly never drawn another connection between Dubos and social ecology since his comment in 1974. Dubos, himself, likely distinguished his position from Bookchin's. Significantly, he never identified himself as a social ecologist in any of his books.

It should come as no surprise then that very few social ecologists actively embrace Dubos' extreme anti-wilderness garden vision. Yet, at the same time, it is also true that many social ecologists do not fully appreciate or share Bookchin's long-standing commitment to a non-anthropocentric ethic and nature philosophy. Bookchin's position on these questions is very influential in social ecology circles, but it is far from a movement-wide norm. In theory and practice, many social ecology activists fall somewhere between Bookchin's more radical philosophical perspective and the more conventional and anthropo-centric approach of the later Dubos.[27]

Like Bookchin and the early Dubos, nearly all social ecologists believe that "both the humanized landscape and the wilderness have a place" in any desired ecological future.[28] However, like the later Dubos, many social ecologists often experience "ambivalent attitudes regarding the comparative merits and rights of the wilderness and humanized environments."[29] Not surprisingly, given the strong anthro-pocentric bias of the dominant culture as well as of conventional Marxist and anarchist theory, many social ecology activists uncon-sciously resolve this ambivalence by excessively privileging the needs and desires of human societies over the interests of other life-forms in "mixed" and wilderness communities. While perhaps not as extreme as Dubos, there is an identifiable extremist garden tendency within social ecology circles. This tendency has inhibited the social ecology movement *as a whole* from developing a normative perspective that holistically integrates radical garden and wilderness visions.

This situation calls into question John Clark's claim that social ecology represents a highly "developed approach to all the central issues of theory and practice" in ecological philosophy and politics.[30] For all of his commitment at the philosophical level to integrating a wilderness vision with his highly developed social vision of a humane and ecological society, even Bookchin has never provided a sustained and searching exploration of how and why to practically restore the balance between town, country, *and* wilderness. His primary intellectual focus, like that of other socially-oriented ecological thinkers of his generation such as Lewis Mumford, E.F. Schumacher, E.A. Gutkind, and Wendell Berry, has always been on restoring the social and ecological balance between town and country—the humanly-inhabited portions of the planet.

Bookchin is not alone in leaving this element of social ecology theory relatively undeveloped. Elaborating a detailed and radical vision and strategy for wilderness preservation has, to date, never taken center stage in any work in the literature of social ecology. In John Clark's recent anthology of social ecology writings, for example, there is not a single article on wilderness preservation.[31] Nor has conservation biology and the preservation and restoration of wilderness ever been a part of the curriculum at the Institute for Social Ecology. It would appear then, that for all of social ecology's wisdom about creating a humane and ecological society, and for all of Bookchin's commitment to a nonanthropocentric nature philosophy, social ecology's practical day to day commitment to wilderness preservation has never been fully developed and it's vision has only rarely exceeded the limited wilderness vision of the mainstream conservation movement.

Whatever else can be said about him, Dave Foreman, the other co-author of this book, has clearly thought long and hard about wilderness. In this respect, he represents a radical alternative to the relatively undeveloped wilderness vision of social ecology. Indeed, since the founding of Earth First! by Foreman and four other disgruntled wilderness activists in 1980, Foreman and the others have launched a powerful philosophical attack on the impoverished wilderness vision of the mainstream conservation movement. In terms as sharp and stinging as Bookchin's critique of deep ecology, Earth First! co-founder

Howie Wolke publicly charged that the reformist conservation movement was guilty of "raging moderation, irresponsible compromise,
knee-jerk Sierra Club dogma, and unknowing (ok, sometimes knowing)
duplicity in the systematic destruction" of wilderness.[32] Foreman went
so far as to argue that the "worldview of the [then] executive director
of the Sierra Club is closer to that of James Watt or Ronald Reagan than
to Earth First!'s."[33]

To these deep ecologists, the tepid wilderness vision projected
by the mainstream conservation movement (as well as by several social
ecologists) amounts to little more than preserving a few minor ecological museums in hard to develop places, maintaining numerous small
wildlife sanctuaries, and protecting some rugged outdoor recreational
resorts. In sharp contrast, the deep ecology movement embraces the
more radical wilderness commitments of Henry David Thoreau, John
Muir, Aldo Leopold, and Bob Marshall.

In June 1983, Dave Foreman and two other Earth First! founders
unveiled the visionary centerpiece of their environmental defense
program, a proposal called the Wilderness Preserve System which
seeks to declare over fifty large wilderness areas in North America
"off-limits to industrial human civilization as preserves for the free-
flow of natural processes."[34] This detailed plan, covering over 716
million acres, was conceived as one component of a larger vision to
restore an ecological balance between town, country, and wilderness
by protecting all remaining roadless public lands over a few thousand
acres. As Christopher Manes reports, these large preserves would
allow:

> no human habitation (except, in some cases, indigenous
> peoples with traditional life-styles); no use of mecha-
> nized equipment or vehicles; no roads; no logging, min-
> ing, water diversion, industrial activity, agriculture, or
> grazing; no use of artificial chemical substances; no
> suppression of wildfires; no overflights by aircraft; and
> no priority given to the safety and convenience of human
> visitors over the functioning of the eco-system.[35]

This stringent plan, already a reform conservationist's nightmare,
does not limit itself to protecting ecological communities within

existing national parks and forests, however. The plan boldly goes on to call for the inclusion of large areas of privately owned and even already "developed" land which could be carefully restored by conservation biologists into a more wild state suitable for inclusion under the Preserve System.

While never believing that their proposal was an acceptable legislative initiative within the current political context, Earth First! pushed the Preserve plan to clearly distinguish itself from reformist environmentalists and to force people to come to terms with its radical ecological vision. Indeed, no group in history, with the exception of the Native Americans who resisted the European invasion of this continent, has ever projected such a sweeping vision for preserving wilderness and, as a direct result, containing and rolling back an environmentally destructive industrial civilization.

Philosophically, Foreman's vision of "Big Wilderness" grows directly out of one of the most basic principles of deep ecology, which, as articulated by Naess and Sessions, affirms that "the well-being and flourishing" of non-human life and its habitat has "intrinsic value" and should be respected by human beings "independent of the usefulness of the non-human world for human purposes."[36] Indeed, most deep ecologists see a commitment to Big Wilderness as a litmus test of whether someone has firmly adopted a nonanthropocentric ecological ethic that transcends mere environmental pragmatism and enlightened human self-interest.

It would be a mistake, however, to think that most deep ecologists are not also mindful of the ecological, scientific, aesthetic, and spiritual benefits of wilderness to human beings and to human civilization. A consistent theme throughout much of the literature, for example, is the cultural value of intimate and respectful human interaction and identification with the wild and its creatures. Following the lead of respected human ecologist Paul Shepard, many deep ecologists point to the growing evidence that psychological and cultural maturity is enhanced and deepened, given our own evolutionary history, by rich wilderness experiences.[37] As deep ecology poet and essayist Gary Snyder warns, "a culture that alienates itself from the...wilderness outside...and from that other wilderness, the wilderness within, is doomed to a very destructive behavior, ultimately perhaps self-destructive behavior."[38]

While deep ecology philosophy does tend to focus primarily on wilderness, it is not necessarily unaware or unconcerned with the ecological and social concerns of human civilization, a fact that has sometimes been lost in Bookchin's critique. Some deep ecologists, in fact, are as concerned as social ecologists with radical social transformation and creating decentralized, non-hierarchical, and democratic bioregional human communities with a dynamic steady-state economy based on eco-technologies and ecologically sound production and consumption practices. As Gary Snyder puts it, "if [humanity] is to remain on earth [it] must transform the five-millennia long urbanizing civilization tradition into a new ecologically-sensitive harmony-oriented wild-minded scientific/spiritual culture...nothing short of total transformation will do much good."[39]

However, this integration of wilderness and garden visions is not necessarily the norm. Just like their nemesis René Dubos, deep ecologists often experience very "ambivalent attitudes regarding the comparative merits and rights of the wilderness and of humanized environments." It is telling that some deep ecologists have chanted "Down With Human Beings!" around campfires at Earth First! gatherings. This is, as Dave Foreman has put it, "an honest expression" of some deep ecologists' perspective.[40]

The wilderness vision can clearly be stretched to exclusive, anti-human, anti-social extremes. Indeed, what first sparked Bookchin's alarm about deep ecology was the publication of remarks by a handful of influential deep ecology wilderness activists which showed a callous disregard for human life and a serious ignorance of the underlying social roots of the global ecological crisis. As Bookchin has noted, the wilderness vision, taken to extremes, "has a less innocent side."

It can lead to a rejection of *human* nature, an introverted denial of social intercourse, a needless opposition between wilderness and civilization...[and] a revolt *against* one's own kind; indeed, a disclaiming of natural evolution as it is embodied in human beings. This pitting of a seemingly wild "first nature" against social "second nature" reflects a blind and tortured inability to distinguish what is irrational and anti-ecological in capitalist society from what *could* be rational and ecological in a free society.[41]

In contrast to social ecologists, who trace the roots of the ecological crisis to the rise of hierarchical and exploitative human societies, many deep ecology activists talk of the human species itself as a blight on the planet. As Dave Foreman has put it, "It is time for a warrior society to rise up out of the Earth and throw itself in front of the juggernaut of destruction, to be antibodies against the human pox that's ravaging this precious beautiful planet."[42] Given this analysis, the primary long-term goal of many deep ecologists is not transforming society but rather drastically depopulating the Earth as if human numbers were all that mattered and the various kinds of societies that people can create are of little or no relevance to the ecological question.

While never advocating active genocide, more than a few deep ecology activists have seriously talked of "letting nature take its course" in depopulating the Earth and have openly counseled people to do nothing to avert such "natural" disasters as famine or epidemic disease. More than one prominent deep ecologist has even advocated active measures such as militarily closing the U.S.-Mexican border to stem the tide of immigrants from Latin America, whom Ed Abbey once described as "morally-culturally-generically" inferior people.[43] All of this has led to a number of feminist and anti-racist critiques of such positions within the ecology movement by such ecological writers as Marti Kheel, Ynestra King, Janet Biehl, Carl Anthony, and the many authors of *We Speak For Ourselves: Social Justice, Race, and Environment.*[44]

While not necessarily the norm, there is clearly a misanthropic strain within the more extreme wilderness visions articulated by some deep ecologists. This blunts the social perspective and ethic of the entire movement and its members. Indeed, the deep ecology movement *as a whole* lacks a consistent or clear social analysis of the ecology crisis or even a consistent commitment to humane social ethics. Anarchistic ecotopian visions coexist with potentially chilling and authoritarian perspectives as well as calls to completely "unmake civilization" and return to hunter and gatherer societies everywhere on the planet.

Dave Foreman is perhaps one of the best individual examples of this wide range of deep ecology social thought. Contrary to countless criticisms of him, however, Foreman has most often embraced a radical bioregional social vision as his chosen goal for the humanly inhabited portions of the Earth.[45] At other times, however, his social thinking has been much more accommodating to the status quo, as if he actually believed that the Earth's remaining wilderness areas could be success-fully protected long-term without replacing the industrial capitalist social system. In his book *Ecodefense: A Field Guide to Monkeywrenching,* for example, Foreman emphatically asserts that direct-action efforts such as Earth First!'s "do not aim to overthrow any social, political or economic system."[46] Even more troubling are a few of Foreman's past comments, particularly those on immigration and famine, which suggest an icy indifference to human suffering similar to the oppressive sensibilities of the very power elites that Foreman has, at other times, called "the thugs who run modern civilization."[47] Foreman's occasional calls for a "return to the Pleistocene" also suggest a wholesale and uncritical rejection of agriculture, technology, natural science, and humanist social philosophy.

Foreman's personal confusion over these social questions and his occasional flirtation with a reactionary and extremist wilderness vision in the name of deep ecology could perhaps be dismissed as an aberration but such positions have been repeated or allowed to go unchallenged by many other deep ecology activists and thinkers. Given this situation, it is little wonder that some deep ecologists adopt an even more profoundly anti-human, exclusive version of the wilderness vision and routinely sacrifice fragile social ethics in the name of enhancing our environmental ethics.

Social ecologists offer an important and needed alternative to these anti-human extremes within deep ecology philosophy and social thought. For one thing, all social ecologists believe that human aspira-tions for creating healthy and democratic human communities are legitimate moral concerns in and of themselves, and a vital interest of our species. In contrast, deep ecologists have very mixed views on the moral legitimacy of these human-centered concerns. While key philos-ophers in both radical tendencies agree on the limits of an exclusive, anthropocentric concern for human beings, social ecologists take the humanistic aspect of their politics very seriously. Most believe that the radical ecology movement ought to articulate and resolutely support a nonanthropocentric, ecological humanism as one essential aspect of its larger moral vision.

The other key insight that social ecology offers to the radical ecology movement is its emphasis on the historic and organic connection between social hierarchy and the ecological crisis. Perhaps the most basic principle of social ecology today is that the social factor most underlying the destructive relationship between human societies and the rest of the natural world is the historic breakdown of community solidarity within early human societies and the resulting expansion of hierarchy, domination, and exploitation within the global human community. This social history, argues Bookchin, has profoundly conditioned "the way we experience reality as a whole, including nature and nonhuman life-forms."[48] Historically, this conditioning fosters anthropocentrism and encourages the very idea of dominating nature.

Given this analysis, it is inconceivable to social ecologists that ecology activists can effectively defend the Earth, in any long-term fashion, if they leave the tapeworm of human oppression firmly embedded within the very guts of our society. For Bookchin and other social ecologists, wilderness preservation, even on the scale proposed by Earth First!, is not nearly radical enough. They argue instead that the essential task, if we are to defend the Earth successfully, is not simply to try to contain ecologically destructive societies but to ultimately and fundamentally transform them.

Can common ground be found between these two wings of the radical ecology movement? When the Federal Bureau of Investigation arrested Dave Foreman on trumped-up charges of "terrorism" in 1989, it became clear that the radical ecology movement is now under heavy official attack. The need for a principled unity among all the wings of the movement, regardless of their continuing differences, became increasingly obvious. In order to counter the traditional divide-and-conquer tactics of the FBI, Bookchin and Foreman accepted the Learning Alliance's long-standing invitation for a joint public meeting in order to show their solidarity, acknowledge the common ground that could be found between them, and explore their philosophical and political differences in a way that showed that deep ecologists and social ecologists can listen to and learn from each other.

The result, as revealed in this book, is a remarkable and thought-provoking rejection of the extremes of both the wilderness and garden visions and a move toward a genuinely integrated radical vision. Not all their differences were resolved, of course. Bookchin and Foreman had to agree to disagree on a number of important topics raised. Yet, the shared contours of an exciting radical ecological politics that integrates the best of the garden and wilderness visions was clear for all to see.

This is a important victory for the radical ecology movement. It reflects the significant movement away from one-sided programs and strategies on the part of many deep and social ecologists. It is heartening, for example, to hear a prominent deep ecologist like Bill Devall finally acknowledge that "Marxist, socialist, and anarchist perspectives can help deep ecologists explore and understand the political and social factors—including the role of capitalism and multinational corporations—involved in the degradation of our planet."[49] It is also encouraging to see new, more socially-oriented, leaders emerge in Earth First! and to see their efforts to build an environmental alliance with timber workers to save old-growth forests and replace the corporate timber companies with environmentally responsible worker-owned cooperatives.

It is equally heartening to see social ecology groups such as the Left Green Network asserting more forcefully than ever that they "stand with every struggle for the protection of nonhuman life...the conservation of species diversity, habitats, and ecosystems, and the expansion of wilderness areas."[50] The long standing social ecology commitment to wilderness is now clearly more than rhetorical. Social ecology groups such as the Earth Action Network not only called for "vastly expanding public parks, wilderness areas and wildlife habitat," they actively helped organize Redwood Summer and are now organizing other "sustained environmental actions involving civil disobedience, direct action, and creative resistance."[51] In Vermont, the Burlington Greens have actively pushed a voter initiative drive for a moratorium on economic development, including development of lucrative lakefront property and ski resorts. They also recently launched a major direct-action campaign against a large biotechnology research firm operating within their city.

A more unified, more holistic, more integrated radical ecology movement may well be emerging. If so, this movement will be neither anthropocentric nor misanthropic. It will seek both to expand wilderness *and* create a humane and ecological society. Its vision will balance creative human intervention in nature with humble and caring restraint. Furthermore, this movement will understand and accept ecological and ethical limits to global economic and population growth while seeking sustainable and just development of all societies. It will also seek to break up the modern imperialist system that ravages one human community to advance the interests of another and, on a more personal level, it will foster the (re)emergence of an ecological sensibility that can ground our lives in a heartfelt sense of connection and communion with the entire world of life.

This book points the way towards such an inspiring movement. Happily, it does so in a way that both deep and social ecologists can clearly understand. The integrative perspective evidenced here builds on the strengths of both schools of thought. This book, of course, represents only a beginning, not an ending. It is just one needed step by two influential activists and thinkers. Other voices need to be seriously considered as well. The larger movement, for example, needs to listen well to eco-feminists, black environmentalists, Native Americans, sympathetic union organizers, and Third World activists.

It would be hard to overestimate the value of this dialogue, however. Together, in this book, Bookchin and Foreman offer provocative and insightful answers to that increasingly important question, "Whither the radical ecology movement?"

Part I

The Dialogue—Winter 1989

Chapter 1

Looking for Common Ground

Murray Bookchin:

I have been a social activist for over 55 years. I was a radical labor union organizer in the 1930s and 1940s, and I was deeply involved in the civil rights movement, the New Left, and the countercultural movement of the 1960s and 1970s. I have also been a longtime activist in the ecology movement. I am pleased, for example, that Roderick Nash set the record straight in his book *The Rights of Nature* by pointing out that I was on the ecological battlefront a long time ago, well before the word "ecology" was even widely used.

Most people do not know that I was on the ecological frontlines as far back as 1952. At that time, I opposed the use of pesticides and additives in food. In 1954, I campaigned against nuclear testing and fallout. I protested the radioactive pollution problems of the "peaceful atom" that became public with the Windscale nuclear reactor incident in Great Britain in 1956 and then later when Con Edison attempted to construct the world's largest nuclear reactor in the very heart of New York City in 1963. Since then, I have been active in anti-nuke alliances such as Clamshell and Shad and their predecessors such as Ecology Action East. More recently, I've done what I can as a member of the Burlington Greens in Vermont and I have helped start a continental Left Green Network that works within the Green Committees of Correspondence. My goal has long been to help build a genuinely radical North American green movement that will harmonize the relationships among human beings and between society and the biosphere.

However, I have never limited my efforts to activism and organizing. I have had a long and vital concern with ecological philosophy and social theory. I do not think it is possible to overestimate the value of thinking insightfully and creatively about defending the Earth. We need ideas, good ideas, to guide our activist work. That is what we have always emphasized at the Institute for Social Ecology which I co-founded in 1974 with Dan Chodorkoff, and which is still going strong today.

In the book by Roderick Nash I just mentioned, Nash maintains that I have "few equals" when it comes to "time spent laboring in the trenches of radical environmental theory."[1] I like to think that this is true. Without sounding too immodest, I have been on the "frontline" of green political thought. Since 1952, I have written over thirteen books on social/ecological theory, including *Our Synthetic Environment*, which came out six months before Rachel Carson's *Silent Spring*, *Toward An Ecological Society*, *The Ecology of Freedom*, *The Modern Crisis*, and, most recently, *Remaking Society: Pathways to a Green Future*. I have also taught over 2,000 students at the Institute and have traveled and lectured widely.

So I urge people: when you feel that you want to be critical of my ideas, and I think that you should, please be good enough to read my writings and listen to what I have to say. I'm getting a lot of critical stuff right now from the academic professorial crowd in which people are criticizing me on the basis of only one or two articles and sometimes even hearsay. I am not asking ask you to read *all* of my stuff, just enough to make a responsible assessment and criticism.

If people do read my work, they will discover that besides having been a labor organizer in foundries and auto plants in a number of big industrial cities, besides having been a revolutionary leftist for over 55 years, I share a good deal of the ecological state of mind of my conservation friends in Earth First!. Does that surprise people? Frankly, I see eye to eye with the activists of Earth First! on a large number of things. In many ways, I think they and Dave Foreman are doing a wonderful job. I feel a very keen sympathy for their many direct-action campaigns to protect wilderness. They are not terrorists as the FBI would have you believe. They are doing important work, work I strongly support.

While support for wilderness preservation is peppered throughout my writings, people may not realize that I am a "wilderness freak." I have not spent all my time on picket lines, in meetings, in my office, or in libraries. My passion for wilderness areas, for wildlife, is a lifelong passion. From my childhood onward, when the Bronx still had some stands of original forest, I loved exploring the wild world. I've been to almost every national forest and every national park in the United States and many in Europe, from the Olympics and the Smokeys to the Black Forest in Germany. I've picked up the Appalachian Trail as far north as Vermont, and as far south as Tennessee. I've hiked it everywhere in between. I couldn't stop heading for the Ramapo Mountains every single weekend for the greater part of two years when I taught in New Jersey. I love those mountains dearly.

Some of the greatest moments in my life have been hiking deep into forest areas in winter alone, where if I so much as sprained my ankle I would freeze to death. My greatest regret now that I am 70 and suffer from a severe case of osteoarthritis is that I can no longer hike in the wilderness. Today, I have to be a more distant admirer. I would physically stand shoulder to shoulder with everyone in Earth First! to defend wild areas if I could. On this score, there is no opposition between Dave Foreman and myself, none whatsoever!

Our society has got to learn to live in peace with the planet, with the rest of the biosphere. We are in complete agreement on this fundamental point. We now live under the constant threat that the world of life will be irrevocably undermined by a society gone mad in its need to grow—replacing the organic by the inorganic, soil by concrete, forest by barren earth, and the diversity of life-forms by simplified ecosystems; in short, by turning back the evolutionary clock to an earlier, more inorganic, mineralized world that is incapable of supporting complex life-forms of any kind, including the human species. The entire world of life, including those few but wonderful wild places that remain, must be protected. Indeed, wild areas must be expanded. Dave and I have no disagreement on this.

I also agree that we need to promote a rational solution to the human population problem. The world's human population needs to be brought into a workable equilibrium with the "carrying capacity" of the planet. Sooner or later, the mindless proliferation of human beings will have to be dealt with. It is absolutely essential, however, that we first clearly identify what we mean by terms like "overpopulation" and "carrying capacity."

This is where the thinking of some deep ecologists frightens me. We need an understanding of the problem that has nothing to do with gas chambers and racism. I know what it means to face the brunt of a "population control" program. All my relatives in Europe are dead. They were murdered in the Nazi Holocaust. They were slaughtered in the name of a "population problem." For Hitler, the world would be overpopulated if just one Jew was left alive.

I've never believed that people in Earth First! are fascists. I am afraid, however, of certain positions and statements, the tendency of which remind me of things I heard fifty years ago when there was a world-wide fascist movement that used "naturalistic" Malthusian arguments to justify racist population control policies. This abuse of the "overpopulation" issue is not just a distant historical issue, either. The abuse of the population issue is ongoing. Just look at what the Rockefeller crowd is trying to do in the Third World. It is a remarkably dangerous question which has to be carefully and rationally discussed if we are to resist racism, sexism, and genocide. Even deep ecologists like Warwick Fox agree that it is "monstrous" to talk of AIDS as a population control measure or, in the name of "letting nature seek its balance," refusing to aid starving children in Ethiopia.[2]

So I ask all of you, everyone in the ecology movement, to please be careful about the population problem. This is a hot issue; a very hot issue. Don't kid yourselves about the objectives of many of those who talk of population control. I went through the 1930s. We paid the price of sixty million lives back then as the result of a racist, imperialist war and mass extermination policy. This sort of thing is not radical ecology. We have to explore this matter carefully and respect the very reasonable fears of women and people of color who have been victimized by population control programs in the past. We have to explore what a humane and ecologically sound solution is. It is important that we unscramble what constitutes the social aspects of the problem from the purely biological ones and to understand how these two aspects of the problem interact with each other. Please, let us be careful. Can we agree on this?

Let me move on to another concern. The ultimate moral appeal of Earth First! is that it urges us to safeguard the natural world from our ecologically destructive societies, that is, in some sense, from ourselves. But, I have to ask, who is this "us" from which the living world has to be protected? This, too, is an important question. Is it "humanity?" Is it the human "species" per se? Is it people, as such? Or is it our particular society, our particular civilization, with its hierarchical social relations which pit men against women, privileged whites against people of color, elites against masses, employers against workers, the First World against the Third World, and, ultimately, a cancerlike, "grow or die" industrial capitalist economic system against the natural world and other life-forms? Is this not the social root of the popular belief that nature is a mere object of social domination, valuable only as a "resource?"

All too often we are told by liberal environmentalists, and not a few deep ecologists, that it is "we" as a species or, at least, "we" as an amalgam of "anthropocentric" individuals that are responsible for the breakdown of the web of life. I remember an "environmental" presentation staged by the Museum of Natural History in New York during the 1970s in which the public was exposed to a long series of exhibits, each depicting examples of pollution and ecological disruption. The exhibit which closed the presentation carried a startling sign, "The Most Dangerous Animal on Earth." It consisted simply of a huge mirror which reflected back the person who stood in front of it. I remember a black child standing in front of that mirror while a white school teacher tried to explain the message which this arrogant exhibit tried to convey. Mind you, there was no exhibit of corporate boards of directors planning to deforest a mountainside or of government officials acting in collusion with them.

One of the problems with this asocial, "species-centered" way of thinking, of course, is that it blames the victim. Let's face it, when you say a black kid in Harlem is as much to blame for the ecological crisis as the President of Exxon, you are letting one off the hook and slandering the other. Such talk by environmentalists makes grassroots coalition-building next to impossible. Oppressed people know that humanity is hierarchically organized around complicated divisions that are ignored only at their peril. Black people know this well when they confront whites. The poor know this well when they confront the wealthy. The Third World knows it well when it confronts the First World. Women know it well when they confront patriarchal males. The radical ecology movement needs to know it too.

All this loose talk of "we" masks the reality of social power and social institutions. It masks the fact that the social forces that are tearing down the planet are the same social forces which threaten to degrade women, people of color, workers, and ordinary citizens. It masks the fact that there is a historical connection between the way people deal with each other as social beings and the way they treat the rest of nature. It masks the fact that our ecological problems are fundamentally social problems requiring fundamental social change. That is what I mean by *social* ecology. It makes a big difference in how societies relate to the natural world whether people live in cooperative, non-hierarchical, and decentralized communities or in hierarchical, class-ridden, and authoritarian mass societies. Similarly, the ecological impact of human reason, science, and technology depends enormously on the type of society in which these forces are shaped and employed.

Perhaps the biggest question that all wings of the radical ecology movement must satisfactorily answer is just what do we mean by "nature." If we are committed to defending nature, it is important to clearly understand what we mean by this. Is nature, the real world, essentially the remnants of the Earth's prehuman and pristine biosphere that has now been vastly reduced and poisoned by the "alien" presence of the human species? Is nature what we see when we look out on an unpeopled vista from a mountain? Is it a cosmic arrangement of beings frozen in a moment of eternity to be abjectly revered, adored, and untouched by human intervention? Or is nature much broader in meaning? Is nature an evolutionary process which is cumulative and which *includes* human beings?

The ecology movement will get nowhere unless it understands that the human species is no less a product of natural evolution than blue-green algae, whales, and bears. To conceptually separate human beings and society from nature by viewing humanity as an inherently unnatural force in the world leads, philosophically, either to an anti-nature "anthropocentrism" or a misanthropic aversion to the human species. Let's face it, such misanthropy does surface within certain ecological circles. Even Arne Naess admits that many deep ecologists "talk as if they look upon humans as intruders in wonderful nature."[3]

We are part of nature, a product of a long evolutionary journey. To some degree, we carry the ancient oceans in our blood. To a very large degree we go through a kind of biological evolution as fetuses. It is not alien to natural evolution that a species called human beings has emerged over billions of years which is capable of thinking in sophisticated ways. Our brains and nervous systems did not suddenly spring into existence without long antecedents in natural history. That which we most prize as integral to our humanity—our extraordinary capacity to think on complex conceptual levels—can be traced back to the nerve network of primitive invertebrates, the ganglia of a mollusk, the spinal cord of a fish, the brain of an amphibian, and the cerebral cortex of a primate.

We need to understand that the human species has evolved as a remarkably creative and social life-form that is organized to create a place for itself in the natural world, not only to adapt to the rest of nature. The human species, its different societies, and its enormous powers to alter the environment were not invented by a group of ideologues called "humanists" who decided that nature was "made" to serve humanity and its needs. Humanity's distinct powers have emerged out of eons of evolutionary development and out of centuries of cultural development. These remarkable powers present us, however, with an enormous moral responsibility. We can contribute to the diversity, fecundity, and richness of the natural world—what I call "first nature"—more consciously, perhaps, than any other animal. Or, our societies—"second nature"—can exploit the whole web of life and tear down the planet in a rapacious, cancerous manner.

The future that awaits the world of life ultimately depends upon what kind of society or "second nature" we create. This probably affects, more than any other single factor, how we interact with and intervene in biological or "first nature." And make no mistake about it, the future of "first nature," the primary concern of conservationists, is dependent on the results of this interaction. The central problem we face today is that the social evolution of "second nature" has taken a wrong turn. Society is poisoned. It has been poisoned for thousands of years, from before the Bronze Age. It has been warped by rule by elders, by patriarchy, by warriors, by hierarchies of all sorts which have led now to the current situation of a world threatened by competitive, nuclear-armed, nation-states and a phenomenally destructive corporate capitalist system in the West and an equally ecologically destructive, though now crumbling, bureaucratic state capitalist system in the East.

We need to create an ecologically oriented society out of the present anti-ecological one. If we can change the direction of our civilization's social evolution, human beings can assist in the creation of a truly "free nature," where all of our human traits—intellectual, communicative, and social—are placed at the service of natural evolution to consciously increase biotic diversity, diminish suffering, foster the further evolution of new and ecologically valuable life-forms, and reduce the impact of disastrous accidents or the harsh effects of harmful change. Our species, gifted by the creativity of natural evolution itself, could play the role of nature rendered self-conscious.

Audience Member:

Excuse me, I want to know what you have to say about the technological fix called genetic engineering? I'm hearing other species, other animals, being spoken about by you as subordinate moments in the evolution of human consciousness, the self-consciousness which you call "second nature." It seems to me that if we choose to believe this about other organisms then there is no reason to resist genetically engineering other organisms to suit our wishes. What kind of spiritual perspective does this represent?

Murray Bookchin:

I have some surprising news for you. I don't believe that human beings are lords over nature and that animals and other forms of life are subordinates. I beg you again, please, read what I have written and listen with care to what I have to say. For years, I have advocated an ethics of complementarity. Complementarity, as distinguished from domination, presupposes a new sensibility that respects other forms of life for their own sake and that responds actively in the form of a creative, loving, and supportive symbiosis.

Let me make it very plain. I don't trust the current scientific establishment to invent a toothpick, let alone tinker with bio-engineering. I believe that we have to bring all of this garbage to an end right now. The current social setup means that the scientific establishment is not *morally* capable of dealing with bio-technology. The truth is, given the current structure of technological innovation, it will put almost anything it creates to some kind of malicious and vicious purpose.

I am not advancing a view that approves of "natural engineering." The natural world, as I have stressed repeatedly in my writings, is much too complex to be "controlled" by human ingenuity, science, and technology. My own anarchist proclivities have fostered in my thinking a love of spontaneity, be it in human behavior or in natural development. Natural evolution cannot be denied its own spontaneity and fecundity. That is why one part of our struggle should always be to protect and expand wilderness areas.

Furthermore, let's completely put an end to the claims that I approve of cruelty to animals. Admittedly, I'd like to see a cure, if possible, to cancer, to diseases that cause pain and so on, but believe me, torturing animals in the name of research is monstrous. It has to be stopped. I just saw a documentary about what they do to research animals. It is unspeakable what a man preparing an MA thesis will do to an animal in order to merely prove that the animal feels pain. Do they have to "discover" that? These are great minds at work indeed! The power to torment living beings has to be taken away from researchers. The current state of affairs is horrible.

So understand that at this moment, where things stand right now, I am practically a Luddite. I should make that plain. Our society is so immoral that it can't be entrusted to invent anything until we are able to sit down and decide, as a socially responsible, ecologically sensitive community, how we're going to design and use our technology. This is not to say that I oppose research or technology, but this society is not morally fit to decide what is necessary or not.

Another way is possible, of course. Eco-technologies can and should be developed. There has been some interesting work in this area during the last twenty-five years. I have personally experimented with various eco-technologies since 1974 at the Institute for Social Ecology. There we put up solar collectors, windmills, ecologically designed buildings; we worked with aquaculture and organic agriculture assisted by a variety of tools and techniques. Other groups such as the New Alchemy Institute have been working on these things even more intensely than we have. I am convinced a liberatory eco-technology is possible. Hopefully, we can all agree on that.

If people do read my work, we can also put to rest the supposition that my outlook is anti-spiritual. This claim is utter nonsense. Anyone who reads *The Ecology of Freedom* will find that it repeatedly calls for a new ecological sensibility, for a new spirituality. There is full agreement on the need for a spiritual connection to the natural world.

The only possible disagreement is whether or not this ecological spiritual sensibility will be naturalist or supernaturalist in orientation.

Since spirituality can mean a decent, indeed, a wholesome sensitivity to nature and its subtle interconnections, it is very important that we keep the ecology movement from degrading this concept into a required or expected belief in an atavistic, simple-minded form of nature worship peopled by gods, goddesses, and eventually by a new hierarchy of priests and priestesses. People who believe that the solution to the ecological crisis is to create a new "green religion" or to revive beliefs in ancient gods, goddesses, or wood-sprites are mystically obscuring the need for social change. The tendency to do just this among many deep ecologists, eco-feminists, and "New Age" greens concerns me. The distinction I make between a needed naturalistic spirituality and an unnecessary, and potentially harmful, supernaturalistic "green religion" is a valuable contribution, I think.

Let me close by saying I believe that there is much common ground between Dave Foreman and myself. As I said before, we should give our support to Earth First! and their direct-action campaigns to preserve what is left of wild nature. Dave is on the frontline on this question and deserves, together with the rest of Earth First!, our full support, especially now when Earth First! is under attack by the FBI.

We cannot let the FBI get away with painting the radical ecology movement as "terrorist." I've been involved in radical direct-action politics all my life. I know what it is like to be attacked by the FBI. I know what a bunch of lunatics they are. People seriously working to defend the Earth will soon find themselves going up against powerful utilities, large corporations, private detective agencies, local police departments, and the FBI. I only wish I still had the physical ability to directly take part in daring nonviolent direct-action campaigns such as Redwood Summer.

I also want to say that I think that many of the political differences between Dave and myself are complementary. Dave and Earth First! work on preserving the wilderness; I and others are trying to create a new grassroots municipal politics, a new cooperative economics, a new pattern of science and technology to go along with their direct action, demonstrations, rallies, and protests to protect wilderness. We need to learn that we are different aspects of a single movement. We also need to try to amicably deal with those principled political differences that do exist between us. There are probably still some major problems between us that have to be explored. Yet, even if we can't straighten them all out, we must at least learn how to better work together on what we can agree on. Our future depends on it.

Dave Foreman:

I agree with everything Murray just said, and I feel like I should just sit down. I'm not sure I have a whole lot more to add. Agreeing with Murray might seem a little strange for someone who started his political career as a college freshman campaigning for Barry Goldwater in 1964. Yet, I really do.

Let me begin my remarks by giving you a little background on my own work and perspective within the ecology movement. I'll leave out, for now, the story of my getting over my brief infatuation with Goldwaterism. All I can say in my defense is that I didn't know at the time that Goldwater stood for paranoid anti-communism and subservience to big business. I thought he was talking about a return to libertarian, Jeffersonian democracy.

Anyway, by the early 1970s I was working as a mule-packer and horse-shoer up in northern New Mexico and getting more and more concerned about what was happening to the national forests up there. Finally, I decided to go back to Albuquerque and try to get a graduate degree in biology and get involved in the conservation movement. I immediately got involved in the U.S. Forest Services's first Roadless Area Review and Evaluation (RARE) program, which turned out to be a horrible farce. I was also studying herpetology at the time and we were supposed to go out and pickle 50 snakes and lizards before the end of the semester. Well, I was studying herpetology because I liked snakes and lizards, so I ended up dropping out of grad school by the middle of the first semester and I have been a professional rabble-rousing conservationist ever since.

I first went to work for The Wilderness Society early in 1973 for $250 a month as their New Mexico representative and I slowly worked my way up until I went to Washington, D.C. in the late 1970s as their chief lobbyist. After going through the Carter administration process, where we got lobbied more than we lobbied them, and where it seemed like the more influence and access we had, the more we compromised,

a number of us began to ask what had happened to the environmental
movement. At that time, newspapers and TV news were reassigning
all their environmental reporters, because the environmental movement was dull. We were also concerned that environmental groups
were becoming indistinguishable from the corporations they were
supposedly fighting. I guess if you organize yourself like a corporation,
you begin to think like a corporation. People who had once gotten a job
in the movement by being active volunteers now were more concerned
with improving their individual careers. They did not want to rock the
boat because they didn't want to spoil their chances of being administrative aide to a senator, or an assistant secretary of the interior at some
point in the future.

     Given our frustration with the conventional conservation move-
ment, several of us who worked for The Wilderness Society, the Sierra
Club, and Friends of the Earth began talking about sparking a
fundamentalist revival within the environmental movement. We
wanted to get back to the basics of John Muir and Aldo Leopold. So on
a camping trip in the desert in Mexico, we decided it was time to quit
talking about how bad things had gotten and actually do something
about it.

     We started Earth First!. Maybe we were all just going through an
early mid-life crisis. I don't know. We sure had fun lowering banners
down the front of the Glen Canyon Dam, making it look like it had
cracked. That was one of our first actions. We were kicking up our heels
a bit and playing the Coyote of the environmental movement. We tried
to do things with a sense of humor. Lord knows most of the social
change movement in this country lacks a sense of humor. This was one
of the things we very much wanted to bring to our work. Perhaps
because of it, Earth First! caught on a lot better than we ever dreamed
it would.

     As we developed Earth First!, we began to explore some tech-
niques of radical organizing. Earth First! originally came out of the
mainstream conservation movement, and that is still where my roots
are, and that is still the audience that I feel most comfortable speaking
to and trying to influence. I think the greatest strength and accomplish-
ment of Earth First! has been our ability to redefine the parameters of
the national environmental debate. Back at the beginning of the Reagan

administration, the Sierra Club was being called a bunch of environmental extremists. Well, we in Earth First! put an end to all that.

Back in those days, there was a spectrum of debate with the
rape-the-land artists over at one end and the "Big Ten" environmental
organizations over at the other. Yet, in an attempt to be credible, proper,
and respectable, the conservationists kept moving over towards the
rape-the-land-artists before we ever even opened our mouths. The
eventual result, of course, was a narrowing of the spectrum of debate,
a narrowing that favored the big industry developers. So, we in Earth
First! tried to create some space on the far end of the spectrum for a
radical environmentalist perspective. And, as a result of our staking
out the position of unapologetic, uncompromising wilderness lovers
with a bent for monkeywrenching and direct action, I think we have
allowed the Sierra Club and other groups to actually take stronger
positions than they would have before and yet appear to be more
moderate than ever. What's different now is that they are compared to
us.

I think that the role of an avant garde group is to throw out ideas
that are objected to as absurd or ridiculous at first, but which end up
trickling into the mainstream and becoming more accepted over time.
We were the first people to talk about the preservation of all old-growth
forests. Before us, no mainstream conservation groups were even
talking about old growth. Now we've got the Audubon Society and The
Wildlife Federation coming in on this issue. We were the first people
to really bring direct action to rainforest campaigns. And now that's
become very much a mainstream activity.

We were pretty clear from the beginning, however, that we were
not *the* radical environmental movement. We only saw ourselves as
one slice of the radical environmental movement. I know I have no
absolute, total, and complete answer to the worldwide ecological crisis
we are in. My path is not the right path; it's the path that works for me.
I think there are dozens and dozens of other approaches and ideas that
we will need in order to solve the crisis we're in right now. We need
that kind of diversity within our movement. In Earth First!, we have
tended to specialize in what we're good at: wilderness preservation and
endangered species. That doesn't mean the other issues aren't important; it just means that we mostly talk about what we know most about.
We work on what moves us most particularly. It doesn't mean that

we're the whole operation, or that we're covering all the bases. We need all the approaches and angles.

I need to emphasize, too, that while I work on those things I know best, on those issues which touch me the most deeply, it doesn't mean that the social problems that Murray mentioned are irrelevant, or that I'm not sympathetic to them. Hell, I've been arrested six times standing in front of bulldozers, or logging trucks, or otherwise fighting giant corporations that are trying to destroy our national parks and our national forests. I think my book *Ecodefense: A Field Guide to Monkeywrenching* is probably one of the most effective little anti-capitalist tracts ever written. I know we are talking radical, anti-capitalist social change here.

One problem I've had in getting the fullness of my message out comes from my impatience at seeing eco-catastrophe going on all around me while so many of those on the left who are always talking about social justice don't seem to even see the problem or care about other species. Let's face it: right now we're in the greatest extinction crisis in the entire three and one half billion year history of life on this planet. Raymond Dasmann has said that World War III has already begun and that it is being waged by the multinational corporations against the Earth.[4] We may lose one-third of all species in the next 20 years because of multinational greed.

I am deeply concerned about what is happening to people all over the world. Yet, unlike much of the left, I'm also very concerned with what's happening to a million other species on the planet who haven't asked for this eco-catastrophe to happen to them. And I have a connection that is very fundamental and very passionate with those other species. I feel a real kinship with them, as well as with members of my own species. And I think, as Murray pointed out, it's very difficult to separate the two concerns. Or, at least, it should be. Regardless of what our emphasis is, regardless of whether it's goose music that plays a symphony to us, or the diversity of people in a vibrant place like New York City that plays a symphony to us, I think we have to recognize that we are on the same side.

Unfortunately for me, when you see this kind of eco-crisis all around you and you react to it, and you begin to suggest some of the things that may happen if we don't wise up and change our way of living on this planet, your ideas may come out as though you're welcoming some of those things. It may come out as though you're saying "ought" instead of "is." I think the problem of the Cassandra is to try to make it very clear that you're predicting certain things because you don't want them to happen, because you want people to wake up. It's not that you're chortling over any suffering. You are compassionate. You are concerned. You're on the side of all the people who are the victims of multinational imperialism around the world. That probably hasn't come out as clearly as it should have in my discussions to date of ecological problems. But it is very real to me, and I'm very concerned about it.

Audience Member:

Mr. Foreman, if you have the slightest commitment to linking issues of social justice with questions of ecological degradation and to trying to find common ground here, how do you reconcile this new tone with your repeated statements in the Earth First! journal that in order to save the ecology of the United States we need to militarily close the U.S.-Mexican border and keep what you call the Latin American hordes from overwhelming us?

Dave Foreman:

I don't think you've ever read anything I've written! I've seen comments circulating like you've described. Ed Abbey has said things somewhat like that, but I've never written anything about militarily sealing the border.[5] Listen, I live in the Southwest. All my relatives on my sister's side are Hispanic. I spend a lot of time in Mexico and have a lot of concern for Central America's problems. I support bi-lingual education and legislation. I have also actively supported the Sandinista revolution in Nicaragua and opposed U.S. foreign policy in the region.

I think, however, that there comes a time when we have to ask some tough questions about whether standard political solutions are going to work. I've looked at what happens to people from south of the border and Arizona, how they're exploited by large corporations. I look at how an open border serves as an overflow safety valve to get rid of dissidents in Latin America and to provide a source of cheap, non-union labor for corporations here at home. And I ask myself, what is being solved by that? I think we delude ourselves when we pretend that somehow by having an open border we're solving any problems in Latin America.

I'm not saying seal the border. I don't think that works. Hell, I'm in complete sympathy with the Central American sanctuary movement. I see the repression and the police state that the border patrol is creating in California. But I think that we delude ourselves when we come up with simple solutions to complex problems. It's not sealing the border and its not opening the border. I think that we will have to solve the deeper problem on a much more multi-pronged basis.

For one thing, it is probably going to require changing U.S. foreign policy. I think if we're going to help solve the social and ecological problems of Latin America we've got to get the CIA out of there; we've got to get United Fruit Company out of there; we've got to get the United States government backed into the position where it can't go in and prop up dictators when their own people throw them out. Our government has done that in Guatemala, in Chile, and it keeps trying in Nicaragua. That is at the heart of most of the problems. As I said before, I'd be happy to join all of you sitting in front of military disembarkation points when they start to invade Nicaragua, which is certainly the most progressive and the most ecological country in Latin America right now, despite the concessions that the U.S. government keeps forcing the Sandinistas to make.

We are all engaged in a battle for life against profit. We are engaged in a struggle for a life of egalitarianism instead of a life of greed and imperialism. We have the same enemies. We are fighting the same battle, regardless of what we emphasize. Gifford Pinchot, the first Director of the United States Forest Service, said there are only two things on Earth, people and natural resources. I think Donald Trump and George Bush would amend that by saying there's only one thing on Earth, natural resources. Ordinary people become just another "natural resource" to the big imperial man. Murray is right. It's one fight.

I must say, however, that for all my intellectual understanding of imperialism, it was directly encountering the repressive power of the FBI and doing a little time in federal custody that really brought home to me the reality of peoples' suffering throughout the world. Personally experiencing a little of the repressive power of the state has a tendency, I think, to create a lot more sympathy for oppressed groups around the world. I certainly have a more visceral appreciation for peoples' suffering these days since the FBI visited me.

From my viewpoint, the FBI effort against me began at about five in the morning on May 30, 1989. A Doberman down the street started barking, so I put my ear plugs in. About two hours later, my wife went to answer the door as it was about to be broken down and opened it up to six men standing there with drawn .357 Magnums and wearing bulletproof vests. They flashed badges at her and pushed her out of the way. They then started running down the hall to our bedroom—they somehow already knew right where it was.

At this point, I vaguely began to come awake as I heard an unfamiliar but authoritative voice yelling my name. I opened up my eyes, still with my ear plugs in, disoriented. May in Tucson is very hot, and I didn't have anything on. And I woke up and there were three guys with bulletproof vests and drawn .357 Magnums standing around the bed. That kind of alarm clock doesn't have a snooze button; you can't go back to sleep for another five minutes. At first I thought, am I on *Candid Camera?* But I realized very quickly that these guys were serious.

I then started thinking about some of the FBI attacks on the Black Panthers, like the FBI/Chicago Police murder of Fred Hampton, who was shot in his apartment while he lay asleep in bed. I fully expected bullets to start coming my way. But being a nice, middle-class honky male, they can't get away with that stuff quite as easily as they could with Fred, or with all the native people on the Pine Ridge Reservation back in the early 70s. So they just dragged me out of bed. They let me put on a pair of shorts, and they hauled me outside.

I did not know what I was being arrested for until six hours later, when I saw a magistrate. Essentially what had happened, we found out, was that the FBI had spent three years and two million dollars trying to frame a bunch of people in Earth First! for trying to create a conspiracy to damage government property. We now know for a fact that the FBI infiltrated Earth First! groups across the country with informers and agent-provocateurs seeking to entrap people into illegal activities. They have amassed 500 hours of tape recordings of our meetings, our personal conversations, and our phone calls. They have also broken into our houses and offices and tried to intimidate numerous ecology activists in several states by agent interrogations and grand jury investigations.

My supposed co-conspirators, three unarmed activists who were arrested by some 50 armed FBI agents on foot, on horseback, and in two helicopters while standing at the base of a power line tower in the desert, were arrested the day before me. Mind you, these three environmentalists were driven to the site by an undercover FBI agent who had infiltrated Earth First!. The whole escapade was largely his idea. He was the only one talking about explosives. I, of course, was nowhere near the "scene" but I was still described by the FBI as "the financier, the leader, the guru to get all this going." I was likened to a "mafia boss" and the other three defendants were described as my "munchkins."

I had only met the FBI infiltrator a couple of times before and very briefly. I couldn't even remember his last name. We had never planned to do anything together. But that doesn't matter to the FBI. Back in the 1970s, the FBI issued a memo to all their field offices telling them that when you are trying to break up a dissident group, don't worry if you have any evidence or facts. Just go in, make a big arrest, make wild charges, have a press conference, and that's what the media's going to pick up. That's the news story. The damage to the group is done. You can always drop the charges against them later. That's no problem. It almost invariably gets less attention in the press. The big lie that the FBI pushed at their press conference the day after the arrests was that we were a bunch of terrorists conspiring to cut the power lines into the Palo Verde and Diablo Canyon nuclear facilities in order to cause a nuclear meltdown and threaten public health and safety.

Essentially what we need to understand is that the Federal Bureau of Investigation, which was formed just after the Palmer raids in 1921, was set up from the very beginning to inhibit internal political dissent. They rarely go after criminals. They're a thought police. And let's face it, that's what the whole government is. Foreman's first law of government reads that the purpose of the state, and all its constituent elements, is the defense of an entrenched economic elite and philosophic orthodoxy. Thankfully, there's a corollary to that law—they aren't always very smart and competent in carrying out their plans.

In this case, I think the U.S. government has made a major tactical mistake, because even the usually compliant mass media are not buying its story. We have gotten some remarkably even-handed press

coverage. I also recently spoke to the Sierra Club international assembly
and had a terrific response. People just aren't buying it. So I'm very
hopeful we're going to overcome this, though we will undoubtedly be
hearing more from the FBI in the future.

Before I close, let me just say that I agree with Murray that the
warped social evolution of our civilization has left us with a very weird
way of looking at reality. I agree a lot with Dave Ehrenfeld, who
characterizes the dominant philosophy of the modern world as being
one where human beings are the measure of all value; where we think
that we can solve all problems, either through technological means or
through sociological means; where we believe that all resources are
either infinite or have infinite substitutes; and where we believe that
human civilization will continue to progress and will exist forever. And
to me, that is stark, raving insanity.[6]

I think there is no reason, divine or otherwise, why human beings,
unless they wake up, will not make themselves extinct. There is a great
deal of madness around us. Julian Simon, for example, is a Republican
economist who said recently that there really are no limits to economic
growth because, after all, we'll soon be able to change any element into
any other element.[7] Therefore, the supply of copper is restrained only
by the entire weight of the universe. I can't even begin to talk to
somebody like that. I mean, we aren't only speaking a different language, we're living on different planets in different dimensions.

And it's that kind of common madness that I think is profoundly
irrational. I talk a lot about being non-rational, about using all sides of
my brain, including the good old reptilian cortex back here. But I think
there is nothing more rational, nothing more sensible than trying to
keep in mind what Aldo Leopold called the first rule of intelligent
tinkering: *save all the pieces.* We aren't saving all the pieces. Species
and whole habitats are being destroyed at a rate unparalleled in the
Earth's history. It is as if we are going through a complicated Swiss
watch with a bulldozer right now.

My own response to this situation is a sort of weird, cowboy twist
on Zen Buddhism. I don't believe in reforming the system any more. I
believe in monkeywrenching it, thwarting it, and helping it to fall on
its face by using its own stored energy against itself. When people talk
to me about the destruction of property, about the evils of destroying
bulldozers, all I can say is that a bulldozer is made out of iron ore. It's

part of the Earth. A bulldozer is the Earth, transmogrified into a monster destroying itself. By monkeywrenching it, you liberate a bulldozer's dharma nature and return it to the Earth.

As I see it, Murray and I, atheists that we both probably are, are trying in various ways to help industrial civilization find its own dharma nature, and become an egalitarian, more tribal society that respects people and respects the Earth once again.

Chapter 2

Ecology and the Left

Paul McIsaac:

Those of you who have been following and reading the Earth First! journal and Murray's writings, or who have attended a number of green conferences have understood that a strident, often harsh, debate has existed within the radical ecology movement for the past few years, a conflict in which both Murray and Dave have played a big part. It seems important to me that they're both here now on the same stage and that they have reached out to each other so strongly in their opening remarks. Perhaps now we can productively turn to a number of differences between them that have appeared in their previous talks and writings. Right now, I would choose just one difference to ask about—their differing views about the role to be played in the ecology movement by what I call, for lack of a better term, the left.

When I was out in Oregon, I had dinner one night with some Earth First!ers and this debate came up within that group. One of the women, Judi Bari, was from the East Coast originally, and comes out of a leftist tradition. When she went out to California, and ultimately to Oregon, she got involved in Earth First!. She is now a very active and successful Earth First! organizer in that area. Interestingly, what she's done with her left tradition is reach back to the tremendous history of the Industrial Workers of the World in the Northwest in order to understand what they did and how they worked, in order to see if their organizing holds any lessons for the radical ecology movement today.

By looking at Earth First!'s organizing situation from a radical working-class perspective, she has come to understand that, if we reduce our consumption of trees, if we stop the exporting of logs to Japan and other Pacific Rim countries, and if we stop the cutting of old *growth, we will create the necessity for retraining workers and even a whole new kind of economy. According to Judi, this requires that Earth First! really address the questions of worker control and creating a decentralized forestry industry that works in a harmonious way with nature. It means thinking about people's jobs and being sensitive to workers' fears.*

While listening to Judi, I noticed that another Earth First! organizer at the table basically had, it seemed to me, a sort of fog that went over his eyes when the dialogue started. In the course of the conversation, it was clear that he didn't understand or want to deal with the left tradition of the Wobblies or feel comfortable with all this talk about the working class. For him, the loggers were immoral, anthropocentrics. They were just as much a part of the ecological problem as the logging companies.

So I ask both of you: does the leftist tradition have anything to offer the radical ecology movement? I know that Dave Foreman has said that the tradition of the radical left is basically a language, a way of thinking, and a way of acting that should be abandoned in order for us to move ahead. Murray, on the other hand, represents the populist, libertarian wing within the left tradition. He calls himself an eco-anarchist. He draws extensively on the left tradition and encourages others to do so as well. Recently, he helped found the Left Green Network to be a self-conscious leftist voice within the broader green movement. What do either of you have to say to this question? What is the value of the left tradition for the radical ecology movement?

Dave Foreman:

Well, I have to admit that I come from a different tradition, a tradition that is actively hostile to the left. As I said, I started out campaigning for Barry Goldwater in 1964. This seemed pretty natural after growing up as an Air Force brat. I was also the New Mexico chair of Young Americans for Freedom during the 1960s. For what it's worth, however, I was in the anarchist faction of YAF. We hated William F. Buckley, that smarmy little twit. Even back then, even when I was a nineteen-year-old YAF punk on the University of New Mexico campus, I couldn't stand William F. Buckley. The guy just turned my stomach.

Yet, at the time, I did buy into the big lie of the Cold War years that there was a global communist conspiracy out there that was threatening to destroy our freedom. The real appeal to me, though, was Goldwater's libertarian rhetoric. You would be surprised at the number of people I've known who worked for Goldwater as college students and have now become radicals.

The Vietnam War started me questioning my beliefs but I had not become questioning enough before I graduated from college in 1968. At that time, you either joined the military or you were drafted. So, I joined the Marine Corps Officer Candidates School at Quantico. I was there at the same time Ollie North was. We never bumped into each other, however. I spent only sixty-one days in the Marine Corps. Thirty-one days were in solitary confinement in the brig.

The Commandant of OCS at Quantico told me I was the worst officer candidate in Marine Corps history, which now seems like a pretty good compliment. The problem was that I found out very quick that there was nothing libertarian or Jeffersonian about the Marine Corps, or the people fighting the Vietnam War. After my discharge, I went back to New Mexico, to my father's great distress. He would have preferred I died in Vietnam rather than dishonor the family (though we have had a rapprochement since). I also became active with the anti-war movement at the University of New Mexico and made several speeches against CIA recruiting and the war. This was a fairly big coup for campus radicals, to have the former leading hawk on the UNM campus come back from the Marines and take the other side.

Since then, I have been in a not always comfortable dance with the left. I share a number of commitments with the left, yet, I come at my politics from a somewhat different direction. For years, my primary political and philosophical tradition has been the U.S. conservation movement. My heros are Henry David Thoreau, John Muir, Aldo Leopold, and Bob Marshall. For all the complaints about my ignorance about the left, a lot of leftists have never seriously grappled with the ideas of these people. Our traditions overlap, sure, but they are also different.

I come from the wide open spaces of New Mexico. I haven't come from the urban centers of the East where the left tradition is so much stronger than in the Southwest. The left tradition is not something I understand that well. Leftists often talk a little different language than me. That doesn't mean we have to fight; it just means we start out emphasizing different things.

I actually think we have a lot to learn from each other. I don't necessarily consider myself a leftist. I don't want to tar that movement with my association, for one thing. But I do have a great deal of sympathy for these movements and I continue to learn from my sometimes clumsy dance with the left.

When we formed Earth First! in 1980, we consciously tried to learn from the strategy and tactics of a number of left social movements. The Wobblies were certainly one group we were drawn to. I even published a Little Green songbook, taking after the Little Red songbook of the IWW. I've talked to Utah Phillips and some old Wobblies; I am really attracted to a lot of what they have to say.

In a place like Oregon, where we are seeing huge multinational corporations essentially practicing a policy of cutting and leaving, a good dose of leftist, anti-capitalist analysis can help us understand the situation. These companies, in their obsession for profit, don't give a damn about community stability or employment. They plan to leave in ten years after they have used up the Northwest forests. They have the capital to move somewhere where they can grow pine trees like corn in Iowa.

I totally agree that we need to get the big money out of the forests and make room for small worker-owned operations. I made such a proposal for the Pacific Northwest four or five years ago. My proposal was to prohibit any logging in the national forests except by small locally-owned companies, preferably worker-owned companies. Furthermore, the plan would have required a certain number of jobs per million board feet both in the woods and in the mills. Right now we are cutting as much timber from the national forests as ever, but the employment, the number of people doing that, is about half of what it used to be. And the reason is automation, because the big companies can make more money that way.

Right now we are cutting something like eleven to twelve billion board feet of timber from the national forests every year, but the large timber companies are sending something like ten billion board feet of barely milled logs to Japan every year. In other words, nearly the entire output of the national forests is going unmilled, unprocessed to Japan. The companies are exporting jobs along with the trees. So, if you want to understand this situation, you need an analysis of multinational capitalism, an analysis of capital mobility and its effects on our communities.

One of my biggest complaints about the workers up in the Pacific Northwest is that most of them aren't "class conscious." That's a big problem. Too many workers blame environmentalists for costing them their jobs. But who is costing them their jobs? It's not the conservation movement to protect the old growth forest that is wiping out jobs in the Pacific Northwest, it's the greed of the multinationals.

We could easily have more employment, more community stability in the Pacific Northwest without cutting any more old-growth forest. But how do you get that across to a lot of workers who have bought into the mentality that the companies have put out for them: that the environmental movement is against them, and that if they're good, if they're obedient, if they resist us, everything will be fine?

The history of the Wobblies and other left-wing union movements undoubtedly has a lot to teach us about organizing with workers. On the other hand, I have some big problems with how the left tends to romanticize workers and only see them as victims. The loggers are victims of an unjust economic system, yes, but that should not absolve them for everything they do. It does not follow from the huge guilt of the capitalists that all workers are blameless for the destruction of the natural world. I think we need to face the fact that industrial workers, by and large, share some of the blame for the Earth's ongoing destruction.

I want workers to resist more, to become a lot more militant and not be such eager and willing slaves to the big companies or believe all of their propaganda all the time. Too many workers buy into the worldview of their masters that the Earth is a smorgasbord of resources for the taking. Indeed, sometimes it is the hardy swain, the sturdy yeoman from the bumpkin proletariat so celebrated in Wobbly lore who holds the most violent and destructive attitudes towards the natural world (and towards those who would defend it). I don't think it is wise to put the working class, or any oppressed group, on a pedestal and make them immune from questioning or criticism.

My biggest problem with the left, of course, is that it has so little appreciation for natural systems and for wilderness and wildlife. Our society, our civilization, has no divine mandate or right to pave, conquer, control, develop, use or exploit every square inch of this planet. At best, the left, if it pays any attention to ecology at all, does so in order to protect a watershed for downstream use by agriculture, industry, and homes. It does so to provide a good place to clean the cobwebs out of our minds after a long week in the auto factory or over the VDT. It does so because it preserves resource extraction options for future generations of humans or because some unknown plant living in the wild may hold a cure for cancer. It does so because nature is instrumentally valuable to human beings. The vast majority of leftists today are still unable to see the natural world as part of the circle of life that deserves direct moral consideration quite apart from any real or imagined instrumental value to human civilization.

Most leftists are for ecological goals such as preserving wilderness and biological diversity only to the extent that we can achieve such goals without negatively affecting the material "standard of living" of any group of human beings. The Earth is always second, never first, in their thinking. This makes many leftists unreliable allies in ecological struggles. The simple fact is that what appears to be in the short-term interest of human beings as a whole—or a select group of human beings or of individual human beings—is sometimes detrimental to the short-term or long-term health of the biosphere (and often even to the actual long-term welfare of human beings). The left, to the extent that it refuses to push for human beings to adjust their way of life to be compatible with the planetary community of life, is part of the problem rather than part of the solution to the ecological crisis.

This is perhaps clearest in most of the left's refusal to admit that there is a human population crisis and that we need to lower human population over the long run. The left puts down all issues of resource scarcity to maldistribution and the venality of multinational corporations. There is much truth in this, of course. There is an unconscionable maldistribution of wealth and the basic necessities of life among human beings that must be overcome. However, even if the problem of equitable distribution was solved, the existence of five billion, seven billion, or eleven billion human beings converting the natural world into material goods and food puts the long-term sustainability of human society into question. Much of the left doesn't understand this simple ecological fact.

Some do, of course. The greens have made the sustainability of human society the cornerstone of their political vision. Yet, from my perspective, this isn't enough. For me, the problem is not just to figure out how to level off human population at a level that can be biologically sustained at equitable levels of consumption. I believe that the ecological community is not just valuable for what it can provide human beings. Other beings, both animal and plant, and even so-called "inanimate" objects such as rivers, mountains, and wilderness habitats are inherently valuable and live for their own sake, not just for the convenience of the human species. If we are serious, then, about creating an ecological society, we will need to find humane ways to arrive at a global population level that is compatible with the flourishing of bears, tigers, elephants, rainforests, and other wilderness areas, as well as human beings.

This will undoubtedly require us to lower our current population level which, even if we succeed at overcoming poverty and maldistribution, would probably continue to devastate the native diversity of the biosphere which has been evolving for three and half billion years. I subscribe to the deep ecology principle that "the flourishing of human life and cultures is compatible with a substantial decrease of the human population and that the flourishing of non-human life requires such a decrease."[1] The left is a long way from incorporating this principle into its thinking. Until that time, the left will be a mixed blessing for the ecology movement, offering both insight and delusions.

I also see problems with much of the left's organizing style. Many radical activists are a dour, holier-than-thou, humorless lot. They also seem too hyper-rational at times. Don't get me wrong. Rationality is a fine and useful tool, but it is just that, a tool, one way of analyzing matters. Equally important is intuitive, instinctive awareness. We can often become more cognizant of ultimate truths sitting quietly in the wild than by sitting in libraries reading books. Reading books, engaging in logical discourse, compiling facts and figures, are necessary and important, but they are not the only ways to comprehend the world and our lives. Furthermore, there is also that old story about how the left forms a firing squad. They stand in a circle and shoot inward. I think that it's unfortunate that instead of fighting the George Bushes and the Exxons, we so often find it easier to argue with people more down on our level and with whom we're more closely aligned.

At its best, Earth First!'s style offers a way forward that the left would be wise to learn from. We aren't rebelling against the system because we are sour on life. We're fighting for beauty, for life, for joy. We kick up our heels in delight at a wilderness day, we smile at a flower, at a hummingbird. We laugh. We laugh at our opponents—and we laugh at ourselves. We are willing to let our actions set the finer points of our philosophy rather than debating endlessly about our program. We are willing to get started now, to make mistakes, to learn as we go.

All in all, I think that what we need in the radical ecology movement is a healthier respect for diversity combined with the willingness to learn from all the different traditions that make up our movement. There is a basis for a common perspective big enough to house our various projects and emphases. I accept the fact that I've got a number of things to learn from the left. Yet, I also believe that the left has a few things to learn from me, Earth First!, and the wider conservation movement. Let's learn from each other.

Murray Bookchin:

Look, I was a leftist long before I was an ecologist. I was in the Young Communist League in 1934. I was part of the "International Communist Conspiracy" that used to scare Dave so much. And, I would add, not without some reason. Stalinism is a vicious ideology, and Leninism is not much better.

Like Dave, it was my personal concern with a terrible war that caused me to question my early political beliefs. The Vietnam War of my generation was the Spanish Civil War, or what I now prefer to call the Spanish Anarchist Revolution. We didn't know it at the time—the Communists presented the Spanish Civil War merely as a heroic struggle between a liberal, left-leaning democracy and a fascist military corps—but the reality of the situation, as I later found out, was that the effort by Spanish workers and peasants to answer Franco's military rebellion was perhaps the most widespread and profound anarchist revolution in history.[2]

Few know this history even today. From 1936 to 1939, before Franco's ultimate victory, a system of workers' self-management was set up in numerous cities including Barcelona, Valencia, and Alcoy. Everywhere factories, utilities, transport facilities, even retail and wholesale enterprises, were taken over and administered by workers' committees and unions. The peasants of Andalusia, Aragon, and the Levant established communal systems of land tenure, in some cases abolishing the use of money for internal transactions, establishing free systems of production and distribution, and creating a decision-making procedure based on popular assemblies and direct, face-to-face democracy.

While we did not know the full extent of this revolution at the time, I, among others, began to discover that the Spanish Communist Party, under orders from Stalin, manipulatively used Soviet material support and sold out the Spanish people's struggle against the fascists because the Communists feared the revolutionary anarchist movement even more than a Franco victory. I won't weary you with the details, but many radicals of my generation saw, to our horror, that Stalinism was ultimately counter-revolutionary. For me, this meant becoming a Trotskyist for a short time. The Trotskyists were the only visible revolutionary left group in New York City that seemed to offer a serious challenge to Stalinism, at least as far I could see.

Ultimately, of course, I became an anarchist. I began to see in anarchism a whole new philosophy and strategy for revolution. Where Marxist revolutionaries focused so much on the factory and sought to "industrialize," and "proletarianize" peasants as a central part of their strategy, anarchism followed a very different path. In Spain, for example, it sought out the precapitalist communal traditions of the village, nourished what was living and vital in it, developed its revolutionary potentialities for mutual aid and self-management, and encouraged it to counter the blind obedience, the hierarchical mentality, and the authoritarian outlook fostered by the industrial factory system.

This line of thinking led me pretty quickly to a leftism much more in keeping with the North American revolutionary tradition. Think for a moment what would have happened in this country if the town-meeting conception of democracy had been fostered as against the aristocratic proclivities for hierarchy; if political freedom had been given emphasis over laissez-faire economics; if individualism had become an ethical ideal instead of congealing into a sick proprietarian egotism; if the U.S. republic had been slowly reworked into a confederal democracy; if capital concentration had been inhibited by cooperatives and small worker-controlled enterprises; and if the middle classes had been joined to the working classes in a genuine peoples' movement such as the Populists tried to achieve. If this North American version of an anarchist society had supplanted the Euro-socialist vision of a nationalized, planned, and centralized economy and state, it would be hard to predict the innovative direction the American left might have taken.

It is this leftist, libertarian tradition that I urge the radical ecology movement to learn more about, to creatively draw inspiration from, and, of course, to build on. I believe, however, that even this tradition is not a sufficient guide for green politics. We still have to develop a truly ecological perspective. Dave is right about this. I couldn't agree more with him in this respect. We can no longer speak meaningfully of a "new" or "radical" society without also tailoring our social relationships, institutions, and technology to the larger eco-communities in which our social communities are located.

The most unbridgeable difference between social ecology and the traditional left is that the traditional left assumes, consciously or unconsciously, that the "domination of nature" is an objective, historical imperative. Following Marx, most leftists believe that the "domination of man by man" is, or at least was, a historically unavoidable evil that emerged directly out of the objective human need to "dominate nature." Liberals, social democrats, Marxists and not a few classical anarchists adopted our modern civilization's dominant view of the natural world as "blind," "mute," "cruel," "competitive," and "stingy." What disturbs me here is the very notion that humanity confronts a hostile "otherness" against which it must oppose its own powers of toil and guile before it can rise above the "realm of necessity" to a new "realm of freedom."

It is this view of nature that allowed Marx to write approvingly about capitalism as a progressive force in history. For Marx, capitalism was a progressive stage in history because it pushed human beings beyond the "deification" of nature and the self-sufficient satisfaction of existing needs which were confined within well-defined bounds. Capitalism, according to many people on the left today, whether they consciously think about it or not, is the historical precondition for human liberation. Let us make no mistake about it: Marx, like most

modern social theorists, believed that human freedom required that the
natural world become "simply an object for mankind, purely a matter
of utility" subdued "to human requirements."[3]

Given this ideological background, it should come as no surprise
that most leftists who do take an interest in environmental issues do
so for purely utilitarian reasons. Such leftists assume that our concern
for nature rests solely on our self-interest, rather than on a feeling for
the community of life of which we are part, albeit in a very unique and
distinctive way. This is a crassly instrumental approach that reflects a
serious derangement of our ethical sensibilities. Given such an argument, our ethical relationship with nature is neither better nor worse
than the success with which we plunder the natural world without
harming ourselves.

I fundamentally reject this idea. Social ecology is a left libertarian
perspective that does not subscribe to this pernicious notion. Social
ecologists call instead for the creation of a genuinely ecological society
and the development of an ecological sensibility that deeply respects
the natural world and the creative thrust of natural evolution. We are
not interested in undermining the natural world and evolution even if
we could find "workable" or "adequate" synthetic or mechanical
substitutes for existing life-forms and ecological relationships.

Social ecologists argue, based on considerable anthropological
evidence, that the modern view of nature as a hostile, stingy "other"
grows historically out of a projection of warped, hierarchical social
relations onto the rest of the natural world. Clearly, in non-hierarchical,
organic, tribal societies, nature is usually viewed as a fecund source of
life and well-being. Indeed, it is seen as a community to which
humanity belongs. This yields a very different environmental ethic
than today's stratified and hierarchical societies. It explains why social
ecologists continually stress the need to reharmonize social relationships as a fundamental part of resolving the ecological crisis in any
deep, long-lasting way. It is an essential element in restoring a complementary ethical relationship with the non-human world.

And let's be very clear about one thing. We are not simply talking
about ending class exploitation, as most Marxists demand, as important as that is. We are talking about uprooting *all* forms of hierarchy
and domination, in all spheres of social life. Of course, the immediate
source of the ecological crisis is capitalism, but, to this, social ecologists

add a deeper problem at the heart of our civilization—the existence of hierarchies and of a hierarchical mentality or culture that preceded the emergence of economic classes and exploitation. The early radical feminists in the 1970s who first raised the issue of patriarchy clearly understood this. We have much to learn from feminism's and social ecology's anti-hierarchical perspective. We need to search into institutionalized systems of coercion, command, and obedience that exist today and which preceded the emergence of economic classes. Hierarchy is not necessarily economically motivated. We must look beyond economic forms of exploitation into cultural forms of domination that exist in the family, between generations, sexes, racial and ethnic groups, in all institutions of political, economic, and social management, and very significantly in the way we experience reality as a whole, including nature and non-human life-forms.

I believe that the color of radicalism today is not red, but green. I can even understand, given the ecological illiteracy of so much of the conventional left, why many green activists describe themselves as "neither left or right." Initially, I wanted to work with this slogan. I didn't know whether we were "in front," as this slogan contends, but I at least wanted to move on to something new, something barely anticipated by the conventional left. Indeed, few have been as uncompromising in their criticism of the conventional socialist "paradigm" as I have been.

However, as time has passed, I have come to see that it is very important that we consciously develop a left green perspective. While the green movement is right to reject a mere variant of conventional left orthodoxy dressed up in a few new environmental metaphors, it is a huge mistake, I think, to fail to consciously draw on left libertarian and populist traditions, particularly eco-anarchism. When greens reject their affinity with these left traditions, they cut themselves off from an important source of insight, wisdom, and social experience.

Today, for example, the U.S. green movement cannot even bring itself to say with one voice that it is opposed to capitalism. Indeed, some locals of the U.S. Green Committees of Correspondence are made up of moderate Republicans and liberal Democrats who talk of "truly free markets," "green capitalism," and "green consumerism" as a sufficient means for controlling the policies of multinational corporations. They talk about running workshops for corporate managers to encourage them to adopt an ecologically sound business ethics. A left libertarian green perspective cuts through this shallow, reformist, and very naive thinking.

The radical left tradition is unequivocally anti-capitalist. A key lesson greens can learn from a left libertarian ecological perspective is that corporate capitalism is *inherently* anti-ecological. Sooner or later, a market economy whose very law of life is structured around competition and accumulation—a system based on the dictum "grow or die"—must of necessity tear down the planet, all moral and cultural factors aside. This problem is systemic, not just ethical. Multinational, corporate capitalism is a cancer in the biosphere, rapaciously undermining the work of eons of natural evolution and the bases for complex life-forms on this planet. The ecology movement will get nowhere if it doesn't directly face this fact. To its credit, Earth First! has done better than most ecology groups in understanding this point.

Furthermore, I believe that the lack of a well-developed, left libertarian green perspective has made too many people in the ecology and feminist movements vulnerable to a "counter-enlightenment" mood that is increasingly gaining ground in Western culture generally. While the growing denigration of the Enlightenment values of humanism, naturalism, reason, science, and technology is certainly understandable in light of how these human ideals have been warped by a cancerous patricentric, racist, capitalist, and bureaucratic society, their uncritical rejection of the Enlightenment's valid achievements ultimately ends up by throwing out the baby with the bath water.

That our society has warped the best Enlightenment ideals, reducing reason to a harsh industrial rationalism focused on efficiency rather than an ethically inspired intellectuality; that it uses science to quantify the world and divide thought against feeling; that it uses technology to exploit nature, including *human* nature, should not negate the value of the underlying Enlightenment ideals. We have much to learn from the solid organismic tradition in Western philosophy, beginning with Heraclitus, and running through the near-evolutionary dialectic of Aristotle, Diderot, and Hegel. We have much to learn from the profound eco-anarchistic analyses of Peter Kropotkin, and, yes, the radical economic insights of Karl Marx, the revolutionary humanist, anti-sexist views of Louise Michel and Emma Goldman, and the communitarian visions of Paul Goodman, E.A. Gutkind, and Lewis Mumford.

The new anti-Enlightenment mood, which declares all these thinkers irrelevant or worse, scares the hell out of me. It is potentially quite dangerous. Anti-rational, anti-humanist, supernatural, parochial, and atavistic moods are a frightening foundation on which to build a movement for a new society. Such perspectives can lead all too easily to the extremes of political fanaticism or a passive social quietism. They can easily become reactionary, cold, and cruel.

I saw this happen in the 1930s. That is why I say that eco-fascism is a real possibility within our movement today. That is why I have criticized several of the misanthropic statements that have been published in *Earth First!;* why I have denounced those few Earth First!ers who stand around campfires and chant "Down With Human Beings;" and why I have expressed dismay over the fact that extreme statements on AIDS, immigration, and famine by some Earth First!ers went unchallenged for so long by deep ecology philosophers such as George Sessions, Bill Devall, and Arne Naess. I agree with Dave that we should respect diversity within our movement, but we should not mistake diversity for outright contradiction. Such views are, at best, unnecessary and, at worst, counter-productive to very dangerous.

Is there really no role in our movement for a humanist ethics? Is there really no role for reason? Is there really no role for an ecologically sound technology that can meet basic material needs with a minimum of arduous toil, leaving people time and energy for direct democratic governance, an intimate social life, an appreciation of nature, and fulfilling cultural pursuits? Is there no role for natural science? Is there no role for an appreciation of a universal human interest? Is it really ecological to go around putting humanity down? Do we really have to replace naturalism with the new supernaturalisms that are now coming into vogue?

Certainly Dave is right that a sense of wonder and the marvelous have a major place beside the rational human spirit. However, let us not permit a celebration of these ways of experiencing the world to degenerate, as happens all too frequently these days, into anti-rationalism. Let us not allow the celebration of nature as an end-in-itself to degenerate into a misanthropic anti-humanism. Let us not permit an appreciation of the spiritual traditions of tribal peoples to degenerate into a reactionary, supernaturalist, anti-scientific, anti-technology perspective that calls for the complete "unmaking of civilization" and the valorization of hunting/gathering societies as the only legitimate way of life.

I appeal to all activists in the movement to stand up for naturalism and an expanded, ecological humanism. This is one of the most important lessons I've drawn from the left libertarian tradition out of which I come. If we are to create a free, ecological society, we will need to learn this lesson and oppose the counter-Enlightenment that has gripped far too many of our would-be allies.

We need a resolute attempt to fully anchor ecological dislocations in social dislocations; to challenge the vested corporate and political interests we should properly call capitalism; to analyze, explore, and attack hierarchy as a reality, not only as a sensibility; to recognize the material needs of the poor and of Third World people; to function politically, and not as a religious cult; to give the human species and the human mind their due in natural evolution, rather than regard them as "cancers" in the biosphere; to examine economies as well as "souls;" to develop a sound ecological ethic instead of getting sidetracked into scholastic arguments about the "rights" of pathogenic viruses. Indeed, unless the radical ecology movement integrates ecological concerns with the long-standing social concerns of the left libertarian tradition such as social ecologists have attempted to do, our movement will be co-opted, undermined, or turned into something dismal and oppressive.

I am glad that Dave is now so willing to carefully pick through the litter of the centuries-long tradition of the radical left for useful insights and ideas. This is a worthwhile project, regardless of all the limitations and problems that are common on the left. My worry, however, is that Dave and other deep ecologist thinkers and activists will continue to eclectically borrow some of the specific programmatic proposals of the left libertarian tradition while ignoring or downplaying the underlying emancipatory, naturalistic, and humanistic logic of this tradition.

Let's face it: specific proposals for decentralization, small-scale communities, local autonomy, mutual aid, and communalism, which deep ecology philosophers such as Sessions and Devall have borrowed from eco-anarchists like Peter Kropotkin and myself, are not intrinsically ecological or emancipatory. Such an outcome depends ultimately on the social and philosophical *context* in which we place such programs. Few societies were more decentralized than European feudalism, which was structured around small-scale communities, mutual aid, and the communal use of land. Yet few societies were more hierarchical and oppressive. The manorial economy of the Middle Ages placed a high premium on autarchy or "self-sufficiency" and spirituality. Yet, oppression was often intolerable and the great mass of people who belonged to that society lived in utter subjugation to their "betters" in the nobility.

A clear, creative, and reflective left green perspective can help us avoid this fate. It can provide a coherent philosophical framework or context that can avoid the moral insensitivity, racism, sexism, misanthropy, authoritarianism, and social illiteracy that has sometimes surfaced within deep ecology circles. It can also provide a coherent alternative to the traditional left's neglect of ecology or its more recent, purely utilitarian commitment to reformist environmentalism.

I am convinced that we will need to "green the left and radicalize the greens" if we are going to effectively defend the Earth. That is why I think this dialogue is so important.

Chapter 3

Radical Visions and Strategies

Linda Davidoff:

I guess I was sent from central casting to be the "mainstream" activist in this important discussion. While I agree with Murray and Dave that the ecological crisis is serious, I am not sure I agree with their strategic approaches for making change. For one thing, I believe in the primacy of electoral reform and working within the system.

I've been lucky enough to be a participant in the creation of a coalition here in New York called Environment '90. Ours is a platform-building exercise which has emerged this year in response to the mayoral election. We believe that the choices among the major candidates and their platforms would make a difference in how things would go next year in our city. So we've pulled together groups and individuals who are active in fighting for a better environment and are trying to come up with a consensus statement on what we hoped could happen as a result of a change in government.

The City of New York has been governed for the last twelve years or more by a school of thought that says the way to deal with our fiscal crisis is to sell, sell, sell whatever's available to the highest bidder in order to bolster the tax base. In the case of New York, what we mostly have to sell, sell, sell is our land and permission to build on it. So groups like mine have been engaged along with other environmental and civic activists in a pitched battle in the administrative agencies, in the courts, in the papers, and on TV. The battle for public opinion is over how high should we build; how dense shall we build; how tall shall we build—how far shall we close down, close in, concrete-ify the city that we all have to live and survive in. Our sense is that these issues matter and that it is worthwhile getting together to try to work out a compre-

hensive and realistic platform that the citizens of our city will feel comfortable with. Our hope is that we can spark a series of meetings and discussions that will lead to a program for the first hundred days of the new mayoral administration.

Murray and Dave probably see this as very tame stuff. Both of them seem to think that our society, indeed our civilization, is "rotten to the core" and that it is unreformable. Well, frankly, I don't believe that our society is rotten to the core. Sure, our society is unjust. Our society is exploitative. Our society is making unwise decisions as an entity. Its institutional parts are not yet fully representative of the public interest and we have to change that. But we live in an enormously stable society, one that changes slowly and reluctantly. I don't see a revolution around the corner, eco-anarchist or otherwise. So, I think we better get good at old-fashioned reformism. That's what makes a real difference in the here and now.

I remember working against a presidential candidate during the Vietnam era who wanted to bomb the Vietnamese back to the Stone Age. I worked instead for somebody who wasn't ready to go that far. It wasn't much of a choice, but it was the only one we were offered in the electoral arena where key decisions are made, and I think it mattered. It was important to work for the less destructive candidate. Because in the end, those of us who wanted to stop the war short of completely destroying Vietnamese society and culture needed to be effective in putting pressure to bear on the government to limit its destructiveness. And we did that. Indeed, we eventually stopped the war. We eventually convinced people in influential positions in our society to pay attention to our views and to respond favorably. That, I think, is the key to political effectiveness.

It is quite possible to work within the institutions that are available to us to make things happen the way we want. The trick is being willing to make effective use of the machinery of government available to us and getting our message across to the general public and government decisionmakers without alienating them. Talk of revolution, using "rotten to the core" language, and refusing to take part in elections, political parties, the mass media, the courts, and lobbying all seem counter-productive to me.

Let me use a more current and local example. At a recent meeting of the West Side Panel, a city/state development planning body, it was

announced that the Panel had modified its infamous "Westway Proposal" to fill in the Hudson River, bore a tunnel through it, and place
high rise real-estate projects on the top along with some park land as
a bone for local environmentalists. The head of the panel announced
to the assembled throng—and there were at least a hundred people in
the room and lots of media—that the panel had decided to forego the
option of a landfill. A murmur spread through the crowd as people
began asking each other how come the option of the landfill was not
being pursued any more as part of the construction that is going on on
the west side of Manhattan.

That "how come" is that some local citizens wouldn't give up.
They were incredibly persistent, dedicating their lives to struggle
against this plan day and night, using the decision-making machinery
of the society that was available to them—public hearings, the press,
and the courts. Here is an example of people intelligently using the
institutional apparatus of society to stop a bad thing from happening—
the filling-in of the Hudson River. Well, it has been stopped and we
think we even have a fairly good chance of negotiating with the West
Side Panel for the creation of a modest boulevard and a splendid park
as part of a Hudson River Greenway that could stand as one of the great
monuments to citizen ingenuity and environmental preservation in
this society.

So I think it is possible to defend the Earth through the utilization
of the available institutional machinery in our society and a willingness
to compromise on some points. We don't reject real-estate development
outright, just the worst, most destructive aspects of urban development.
That doesn't mean that we are never militant. That doesn't mean that
we never pose choices in very stark ways. But I think that we have got
to assume that this is a stable society that moves slowly and that we
can change it if we're very, very careful to work out effective, realistic
strategies that have some chance of success rather than chasing after
utopian dreams.

My question for Dave and Murray, then, is why don't you try to
work within the system more? Why are you so convinced that our
society is "rotten to the core?" Why do you see your more radical
strategies for change as realistic? What is wrong with a pragmatic
reformist strategy?

Dave Foreman:

Like everything else, I think that we have to defend the Earth in a lot of different ways. I am not telling people to do only one thing, to use only one tactic or approach. In one sense, I don't care how people choose to defend the Earth—whether they write letters to the editor, recycle newspapers, canvass for an environmental candidate, blockade nuclear power plants with a few thousand other people, or spike trees and sabotage bulldozers alone in wild areas.

I do care, however, that people get off their butts in front of the TV set and do something. You have got to take responsibility for your life and the world. You have got to do something to pay your rent for the privilege of inhabiting this beautiful, blue-green, living Earth. If more people would simply get off their butts and do something, we would have a far better chance of survival and defending the Earth and its many species.

However, I don't think that the goals and strategies that we choose are all equally valuable or effective. Besides getting off our butts, we have got to think hard and figure out what goals and strategies best defend the Earth. I certainly have more questions than answers about this, but a few things seem clear to me. For one thing, I think the moderate and so-called pragmatic approach outlined so well by Linda is limited and frequently counter-productive.

I would be the last one to say that electoral politics, court challenges, and lobbying for good legislation have no place in the tactics of our movement. I think such tactics can be effective and should not be rejected out of hand. As I said before, I used to work at The Wilderness Society as their lobbying coordinator in Washington, D.C. I was also the New Mexico Chair of Conservationists for Carter in 1976. Even though Jimmy Carter's public lands policies led to the formation of Earth First!, he did some good things while in office. That can't be denied. I have also spent many hours negotiating with the U.S. Forest Service and taking part in the public hearings that have been a part of their planning process. Out of this experience, however, I have become convinced that these tactics, by themselves, are simply not effective or practical enough to defend the existing roadless areas that are in such danger today.

At a minimum, you would think that the public lands conservation movement would aim, as one of its most important goals, at keeping industrial "civilization" out of the few wild places that remain. Yet, the mainstream movement has become so loyal a courtier to the dominant industrial order that it cannot even effectively defend this limited goal. You can see the pattern of their current strategy as early as 1956, when conservationists accepted a compromise on the Colorado River Storage Act which cancelled a huge dam on the Green and Yampa Rivers in Dinosaur National Monument by agreeing to one on the Colorado River at Glen Canyon. Today the conservation movement's strategy is to bargain away huge portions of the wild world in order to protect a dwindling core of "untouchable" wilderness areas. This gets us nowhere.

Sure, the mainstream conservation movement's efforts at electoral politics, lobbying, and court battles slow the encroachment process down, but they do not ultimately halt it, let alone reverse it. Let's face it, our representative democracy has broken down. Our government primarily represents the big money boys and stacks the deck against reform movements. Playing only by the system's rules limits you. That is why the reformist conservation movement doesn't even think it is realistic to try to defend all of the remaining wilderness in the United States, let alone expand wilderness areas through ecological restoration. Trying to fit in, to not seem radical or extreme, to always seek compromise obviously keeps you pretty damn manageable. It is no wonder that the mainstream conservation movement has been outmaneuvered over the last fifteen years because of its timid vision and tactics.

For example, in the early summer of 1977, the U.S. Forest Service began an 18-month-long inventory and evaluation of the remaining roadless and undeveloped areas in the national forests which are eligible by law for congressional consideration as protected wilderness preserves. All in all, there were some 80 million acres in the national forests retaining a significant degree of natural diversity and wildness. Along with the national parks and monuments, national wildlife refuges, existing wilderness areas and some state lands, these roadless areas represent the remaining wilderness in the United States. These are the places that hold North America together, that contain the genetic information of life, that represent natural sanity in a whirlwind of industrial madness.

Now you need to remember that from its very beginning the U.S. Forest Service has viewed the national forests as an arena for industrial logging, grazing, mineral and energy development, road-building, and motorized recreation. It should not come as a surprise, then, that in January of 1979 the Forest Service announced the following results of its wilderness assessment: out of the 80 million remaining acres of undeveloped lands in the national forests, only 15 million acres were recommended for protection against logging, road building, and other "developments." In the big-tree state of Oregon, for example, only 370,000 acres were proposed for wilderness protection out of the remaining 4.5 million acres of roadless, uncut forest lands. Of the areas nationally slated for protection, most areas were too high, too dry, too cold, too steep to offer much in the way of "resources" to the loggers, miners, and grazers. Those roadless areas with critical old-growth forest values were allocated for the sawmill. Important grizzly bear habitat in the northern Rockies was tossed to the oil industry and the loggers. Off-road-vehicle fanatics and the landed gentry of the livestock industry won out in the Southwest and Great Basin.

Unfortunately, the response of the conservation movement was not to call for the preservation of the last remaining wilderness lands in their entirety or to use every legitimate tactic at their disposal to protect these lands and resist government and corporate encroachment on wild public lands. Instead, the conservation movement sought to be realistic and compromise, trading most of the wilderness away, in exchange for a marginal increase in the amount of proposed acreage to be legally protected. Because of the very limited nature of their goals, these tactics were ultimately effective in achieving this objective, though even this was a big struggle. But it should be remembered that this achievement was hardly a significant victory for wilderness.

Furthermore, the Forest Service has since come up with a plan that will effectively block any future conventional efforts at expanding the acreage of protected wilderness in the national forests. Generally, only roadless areas are considered for wilderness protection within the national forests. During the 1980s, the Forest Service developed and began implementing a 15-year plan to get rid of the remaining roadless areas by building over 75,000 miles of new road within the national forests. This immense road network (enough to encircle the planet three times) will cost the American taxpayer over three billion dollars to provide large timber corporations access to a mere 500 million dollars worth of timber. More importantly, it will cause a considerable decline in the biological integrity of this country's remaining wilderness areas and destroy these areas' ability to support a huge variety of plant and animal species.

It would appear that the U.S. Forest Service folks consciously and deliberately sat down and asked themselves, "How can we keep from being plagued by conservationists and their damned wilderness proposals?" Their plans seem to be working out quite well. The Forest Service today is systematically destroying unprotected, roadless areas through a massive road-building campaign. The result is that the effectiveness of conventional political lobbying and electoral work to protect wild lands is evaporating and in half a decade the saw, the bulldozer, and the drill will devastate most of what is now wild but legally unprotected. The battle for wilderness by conventional means will soon be over. Perhaps three percent of the United States will be more or less protected and it will be open season on the rest.

Ironically, the conventional political tactics that Linda calls our strongest, most pragmatic, most effective weapons for making reforms in the here and now cannot even protect what little natural landscape we have left in this country, a very minimal goal from my perspective. This is why I believe that a truly effective, wilderness preservation strategy needs to include a large dose of uncompromising, nonviolent direct action and resistance. I think electoral politics, legislation, those mainstream approaches can still play a crucial part, but nonviolent direct action also has to be an important means of defending the wilderness. I say let's approach the problem by looking for the weaknesses in the system, the places where we can throw the wooden shoe in the gears of the machinery, or where we can put the handcuffs on an agency and take power away from them. We need a campaign of resistance whenever and wherever the dying industrial empire tries to invade the remaining wilderness. We need to delay, resist, and thwart the current system using *all* the tools available to us. Sure, this includes filing appeals and lawsuits as well as encouraging legislation that ties the hands of corporations and agencies like the U.S. Forest Service. However, to truly get the job done, we will also need to demonstrate, engage in mass nonviolent civil disobedience, and, frankly, illegally monkeywrench and sabotage wilderness-destroying projects. It is now time for women and men, individually, in small groups, and in large public movements to develop a widely-dispersed, strategic movement of nonviolent resistance against wilderness destruction all across the land.

I believe that such a campaign of resistance can be effective in stopping timber-cutting, road-building, overgrazing, oil and gas exploration, mining, dam building, powerline construction, off-road-vehicle use, trapping, ski area development and other forms of destruction of the wilderness as well as cancerous suburban sprawl. I believe such campaigns can be effective because such campaigns hit the rape-the-land artists where they live—in their pocket books.

Many of the projects that are encroaching on roadless wilderness areas are economically marginal. The profit margins on such activities are real but they are very vulnerable to cost overruns. It is very costly for the Forest Service, timber companies, oil companies, mining companies and others to scratch out the "resources" in these last wild areas. A broad resistance strategy can make it even more costly, perhaps prohibitively expensive. The rising cost of repairs, the hassle, the delay, the down-time caused by "on-the-ground" wilderness resistance activities as well as the loss of public support and the rise of consumer boycotts, strikes, and other forms of community resistance could protect millions of acres of wilderness far more effectively than any congressional act.

Such "extreme" and "uncompromising" actions are not pointlessly "utopian." They are strategically sound. They are pragmatic. Such tactics do, however, require a greater degree of personal involvement and risk than working within normal channels. It takes courage to put your body between the machine and the wilderness, to stand before the chainsaw or the bulldozer or the FBI. More of us need to stand before the mad machine as Valerie Wade did in climbing 80 feet high into an ancient Douglas Fir to keep it from being cut down, or as Howie Wolke did in pulling up survey stakes along a proposed gas exploration road in prime elk habitat.

Sure, both of these Earth First! activists put their lives in jeopardy and both went to jail. Yet I am reminded of the famous story about Henry David Thoreau being sent to jail for refusing to pay his poll tax to protest the U.S. war against Mexico. When Ralph Waldo Emerson came to bail him out, Emerson called through an open window and said, "Henry, what are you doing in there?" Thoreau quietly replied, "Ralph, what are you doing out there?" We need that kind of courage and spirit in our movement today.

Conventional efforts at reform are certainly safer and they are, in some ways, better rewarded. By staying within normal channels you can usually avoid serious political repression. You are also validated rather than vilified. The effect of this validation, however, is to dampen the effectiveness of a movement. I suspect that it is basic human nature to want to be accepted by the social milieu in which you find yourself. It hurts to be dismissed by the official arbiters of opinion as "nuts," "terrorists," "wackos," or "extremists." I think much of the desire to be "moderate" and "pragmatic" grows out of the understandable desire to gain credibility or legitimacy with the media and the political and economic leaders currently running our society.

The American political system is very effective at co-opting and moderating dissidents by giving them attention and then encouraging them to be "reasonable" so their ideas will be taken "more seriously." Appearing on the evening news, testifying before congressional hearings, or getting a job with some government agency are just some of the methods used by the establishment to entice one to share key assumptions of the dominant worldview and to enter the negotiating room to compromise with madmen who are destroying everything pure and beautiful. Take a look at much of the mainstream conservation movement today. The political vision of most of these reformers includes, at a minimum, a global population of ten to twelve billion human beings, nation-states, multinational corporations, the private automobile, and people in business suits on every continent. Such a limited vision is not going to spark or lead a movement for the creation of a wilderness-loving and egalitarian society.

Indeed, such a limited vision has little or no future. Modern society is a driverless hot rod without brakes going 90 miles an hour down a dead-end alley with a brick wall at the end. We do not live in a stable society. We're in the most volatile society that has ever existed on this planet. I think the shit is going to hit the fan in my lifetime; that the greed, the insanity, the domination of nature and human beings, this whole madness is going to come to a head. I think that terrible things will happen in the not-so-distant future that will make the current social and ecological crisis seem like the good old days. To seek only "realistic" reforms, to use only conventional means of social change at this point in time, really means giving up the fight. Reforms that are realistic within the current distribution of institutional power simply cannot take us from here to where we need to be.

In many ways, Earth First! represents a fundamentalist revival within the wilderness/wildlife preservation movement, a return to basics and a reaction against reformist co-optation and compromise. Over the last several decades, as the conservation movement has grown in prominence, Aldo Leopold's now famous "Land Ethic" has been replaced with "political pragmatism." It has dramatically limited its political vision. It now views the entire question of wilderness preservation and species diversity as purely a question of pragmatically balancing competing special interest groups and working out compromises between giant economic interests and public recreation enthusiasts. Earth First! takes the stand that wilderness preservation is an ethical question, a moral question. It can't be simply reduced to the conventional political currency of self-interest, or even the more humanistic concern for human sustainability.

As Ed Abbey frequently said, human beings have a right to be here, but not everywhere, not all at once, not all in the same place. Human society has stepped beyond the bounds; we are destroying the very processes of life. Wilderness is more than puny little backpacking parks in areas with little or no "development" potential. Wilderness areas are the arena for natural evolution, and must be large enough so natural forces can have free rein. There must be vast areas in every bioregion that are off-limits to human habitation and economic activity. These areas must simply be left alone to carry on the important work of spontaneous natural evolution.

This is a radical vision to be sure, one which calls many of our social assumptions into question. Yet, any reasonable policy, given the level of wilderness destruction to date, requires much more than the containment of the current encroachments of "civilization" onto existing public wilderness reserves. It is our job, as defenders of the Earth, to reclaim much of the now asphalted land, the barren fields, ripped forests, and silent mountains. One of the centerpieces of every ecology group's platform should be to protect or create a big core wilderness preserve in every region. Other wilderness preserves, both large and small, should also be established and protected throughout each region as well as wilderness corridors to allow for the free flow of genetic material between them and the wilderness preserves in other bioregions.

Of course, we will need human management and intervention to help nature restore a suitably large area in each region, at least a million acres, to wildness. If certain native animals have been extirpated, they must be reintroduced. If possible, grizzly, wolf, cougar, jaguar, bison, elk, moose, otter, wolverine all must find a home in our public lands again. If salmon streams must be repaired, clearcuts rehabilitated, prairies replanted, roads removed—then that becomes one of the key tasks of ecological restoration.

This is a truly revolutionary ecological vision. Any genuinely effective movement to respond to the ecology crisis will require us to mount widespread nonviolent resistance campaigns, including strategic monkeywrenching, to protect as much wilderness as possible from destruction. It will also will require us to challenge the government, the corporations, and the people as a whole with an ethical vision of Big Wilderness.[1] Yet, frankly, even this is not enough. The radical ecology movement also needs to do the important work of organizing the new ecological society that will emerge out of the ashes of the old industrial empire.

Some of this work may not even seem radical or revolutionary at first glance, but it is. For example, I think the people who are developing cheap and simple low-tech gizmos like solar cookers are doing some of the best work on the planet. These people are saving trees in the Third World by decreasing the demand for wood as fuel. I think their work is profoundly revolutionary because it is also saying that big is not necessarily better, that we don't need big corporate/government techno-solutions, and that people can solve some of their problems on their own. We owe much to the alternative technology movement which has been experimenting over many years with composting toilets, organic gardens, handicrafts, recycling, solar collectors, wind generators, and solar cookers.

Yet these people, like me, are just one piece of the puzzle. If high-tech techno-fixes aren't going to get to the root of the problem, low-tech techno-fixes aren't going to do the job by themselves either.

We must also directly challenge current social institutions on a political and economic level. For instance, we need to make sure that the so-called developed world stops treating Third World people and land as mere resources to be exploited.

We in the United States clearly have a responsibility to resist the efforts of multinational corporations and First World governments to force Third World societies to produce export cash crops for consumption in the First World instead of producing subsistence crops for their own people. This is not just a matter of elemental social justice, it is a key requirement in overcoming the global ecological crisis. Plantation-style, single-crop, export agriculture is far more damaging to the natural world than small-scale, diversified, subsistence agriculture for local and regional consumption. This is but one example of how we need to fundamentally reorganize how we make a life on the portion of the planet that we do inhabit.

Besides the emergence of Earth First!, I think the most encouraging development in North America of late has been the bioregional movement. Bioregionalism is fundamentally concerned with reinhabiting the land in decentralized, egalitarian, and ecologically sound ways. It is a concept far removed from the way of life currently common in almost all suburbs, cities, and farms on this continent. Reinhabitation stresses creatively adapting human communities to the natural region they inhabit instead of single-mindedly adapting the place to an exploitative human society. It means self-consciously and respectfully becoming part of the food chain, the water cycle, the environment of a particular natural region, instead of imposing an exclusively human-centered, global industrial order on the same area.

So while I work very hard to try to prevent the mad thrashing of the dying industrial Storm Trooper from destroying everything beautiful on this earth, I'm glad there are people like Murray in the greens, in the bioregional movement, in projects like the Green City Program in San Francisco, who are trying to create the new society that will come after us. That's their job. It's as important as my job is. My job is more limited. I'm trying to protect as much as possible from the dollar, from destruction in the last days of industrial society. I think Murray and others, in turn, are laying out the concepts and working out the practicalities of a sustainable ecological society that can come after it.

In closing, let me just say, I very much agree with Murray that this society is rotten to its core. I think it's so fundamentally destructive that it's ultimately unreformable in any conventional sense. I simply can't get from here to where I want to be through the strategic approach outlined by Linda. Indeed, it may not take us far enough to even ensure the continued existence of most of the Earth's species, including human beings. A genuinely radical vision and strategy may not succeed either, but I am convinced that it is the best shot that we have got.

Murray Bookchin:

I couldn't agree with Dave more. No doubt there are still real differences between us. Yet, so far as these issues of vision and strategy are concerned, we seem to be in considerable agreement.

To begin with, I share Dave's sense of urgency. Capitalist society, whether in Western corporate or Eastern bureaucratic forms, is fundamentally destructive. The power of this society to destroy has reached a scale unprecedented in the history of humanity—and this power is being used, almost systematically, to wreak havoc upon the entire world of life and its material bases. In nearly every region, air is being befouled, waterways polluted, soil washed away, the land desiccated, and wildlife destroyed. Coastal areas and even the depths of the sea are not immune to widespread pollution. More significantly in the long run, basic biological cycles such as the carbon cycle and nitrogen cycle, upon which all living things depend for the maintenance and renewal of life, are being distorted to the point of irreversible damage. The proliferation of nuclear reactors in the United States and throughout the world—some 1,000 by the year 2000 if the powers-that-be have their way—have exposed countless millions of people and other life forms to some of the most carcinogenic and mutagenic agents known. Some of these terrifying threats, like radioactive wastes, may be with us for hundreds of thousands of years.

To these radioactive wastes we also must add long-lived pesticides, lead residues, and thousands of toxic or potentially toxic chemicals in food, water, and air; the expansion of cities into vast urban belts, with dense concentrations of populations comparable in size to entire nations; the rising din of background noise; the stresses created by congestion, mass living, and mass manipulation; the immense accumulations of garbage, refuse, sewage, and industrial wastes; the congestion of highways and city streets with vehicular traffic; the profligate destruction of nonrenewable resources; the scarring of the earth by real estate speculators, mining and lumbering barons, and highway construction bureaucrats. Our lethal insults to the biosphere have wreaked a degree of damage in a single generation that exceeds the damage inflicted by thousands of years of human habitation on this planet. If this tempo of destruction is borne in mind, it is terrifying to speculate about what lies ahead in the generations to come.

In the face of such a crisis, efforts for change are inevitable. Ordinary people all over the globe are becoming active in campaigns to eliminate nuclear power plants and weapons, to preserve clean air and water, to limit the use of pesticides and food additives, to reduce vehicular traffic in streets and on highways, to make cities more wholesome physically, to prevent radioactive wastes from seeping into the environment, to guard and expand wilderness areas and domains for wildlife, to defend animal species from human depredation. The single most important question before the ecology movement today, however, is whether these efforts will be co-opted and contained within the institutional bounds of "reasonable" dissent and reformism or whether these efforts will mature into a powerful movement that can create fundamental, indeed revolutionary, changes in our society and our way of looking at the world.

I have long argued that we delude ourselves if we believe that a life-oriented world can be fully developed or even partially achieved in a profoundly death-oriented society. U.S. society, as it is constituted today, is riddled with patriarchy and racism and sits astride the entire world, not only as a consumer of its wealth and resources, but as an obstacle to all attempts at self-determination at home and abroad. Its inherent aims are production for the sake of production, the preservation of hierarchy and toil on a world scale, mass manipulation and control by centralized, state institutions. This kind of society is inexorably counterposed to a life-oriented world. If the ecology movement does not ultimately direct its main efforts toward a revolution in all areas of life—social as well as natural, political as well as personal, economic as well as cultural—then the movement will gradually degenerate into a safety valve for the established order.

Conventional reform efforts, at their best, can only slow down but they cannot arrest the overwhelming momentum toward destruction within our society. At their worst, they lull people into a false sense of security. Our institutional social order plays games with us to foster this passivity. It grants long-delayed, piecemeal, and woefully inadequate reforms to deflect our energies and attention from larger acts of destruction. Such reform measures hide the rotten core of the apple behind an appealing and reassuring artificially-dyed red skin.

Ultimately, however, the key problem with the "pragmatic" political strategy of trade-offs, compromises, and lesser-evil choices is not that it can't take us as far as we want to go. An even more sinister effect of this strategy is that it conditions us to go where we do not want to go.

This "pragmatic" approach has had deadly consequences over the course of recent history. Fascism made its way to power in Germany, in part, because the radical labor movement moderated its revolutionary politics and sought to be "effective" by throwing its weight behind lesser-evil candidates. The movement thus surrendered its own initiative and leadership. Such a "realistic" approach, which seemed so practical at the time, led the German workers from making "realistic" choices between a moderate left and a tolerant center, to a tolerant center and an authoritarian right, and finally between the authoritarian right and totalitarian fascism. Not only did this moral devolution occur almost inevitably on a parliamentary level; a cruel dialectic of political degeneration and moral decomposition also occurred within the German labor movement itself. That the once militant and well-organized German working class permitted this political drift from one lesser evil to another without any act of direct resistance is perhaps the most dismal event in its history.

Environmental movements have not fared much better when they have placed their hopes on the nation-state and lesser-evil strategies. To the extent that European environmentalists have entered into national parliaments seeking state power as greens, they have generally attained little more than public attention for their self-serving parliamentary deputies and achieved very little to arrest environmental decay. As Dave so eloquently pointed out, well-meaning environmentalists committed to strategies such as these have bartered away entire forests for token reserves of trees. Vast wilderness areas have been surrendered for relatively small national parks. Huge stretches of coastal wetlands have been exchanged for a few acres of pristine beaches. This is the inevitable result of "working within the system" when the system is *fundamentally* anti-ecological, elitist, and stacked against you.

The coalition of the German Greens with a Social Democratic government in the state of Hesse, for example, ended in ignominy in the mid-1980s. Not only did the "realist wing" of the German Green party taint the movement's finest principles with compromises, it also made the party more bureaucratic, manipulative, and "professional." The result? A once grassroots, radical green movement was changed fundamentally and the state it sought to influence did not. The German Greens seem very far today from their early promise of representing a genuinely new ecological politics.

Let me make it clear, however, that by counterposing reform environmentalism to the possibility of a truly radical ecology movement, I am not saying that we should desist from opposing the construction of nuclear power plants or highways today and sit back passively to await the coming of an ecological millenium. To the contrary, the existing ground must be held on to tenaciously, everywhere along the way. We must try to rescue what we still have so that we can at least reconstitute society with the least polluted and least damaged environment possible. To be effective, however, we must break away from conventional reformism and energetically adopt much more powerful nonviolent direct-action resistance strategies. Furthermore, we need to go well beyond tinkering with existing institutions, social relations, technologies, and values and begin to fundamentally transform them. This doesn't mean that we don't organize around a minimum program with clear immediate objectives or even that we never participate in local elections. I have argued for such measures in my books and articles on libertarian municipalism.[2] It does mean, however, that the immediate goals we seek and the means we use to achieve them should orient us toward the radical fundamental changes that are needed instead of towards co-optation and containment within the existing, hopelessly destructive system.

I am convinced that we will fail to keep our political bearings and avoid co-optation unless we develop a bold and uncompromising vision of a truly ecological future. The highest form of realism today can only be attained by looking beyond the given state of affairs to a constructive vision of what should be. It is not good enough to merely look at what could be within the normal institutional limits of today's predatory societies. This will not yield a vision that is either desirable or sufficient. We cannot afford to be content with such inherently compromised programs. Our solutions must be commensurate with the scope of the problem. We need to muster the courage to entertain radical visions which will, at first glance, appear "utopian" to our cowed and domesticated political imaginations.

Today, we have a magnificent repertoire of new ideas, plans, technological designs, and working data that can give us a graphic picture of the necessary contours of a sustainable and ecological society. Dave has painted half the picture with his vision of restoring large wilderness areas throughout the continent. But what about those areas that are still to be inhabited by human beings? How can they be organized ecologically? Certainly they cannot remain dominated by sprawling urban areas, massive industrialization, and giant corporate farms run like food factories. Such institutional patterns not only make for destructive social conflict, individual anonymity, and centralized power; they also place an impossible burden on local water resources, the air we breathe, and all the natural features of the areas which they occupy.

One of our chief goals must be to radically decentralize our industrialized urban areas into humanly-scaled cities and towns artfully tailored to the carrying capacities of the eco-communities in which they are located. We need to transform the current pattern of densely populated urban sprawl into federations of much smaller cities and towns surrounded by small farms that practice diversified, organic agriculture for the local area and are linked to each other by tree belts, pastures and meadows. In rolling, hilly, or mountainous country, land with sharp gradients should be left covered by timber to prevent erosion, conserve water, and support wildlife. Furthermore, each city and town should contain many vegetable and flower gardens, attractive arbors, park land, and streams and ponds which support fish and aquatic birds. In this way, the countryside would not only constitute the immediate environs of the city but would also directly infuse the city. Relatively close by, sizable wilderness areas would safely co-exist with human habitats and would be carefully "managed" to enhance and preserve their evolutionary integrity, diversity, and stability.

By decentralizing our communities, we would also be able to eliminate the present society's horribly destructive addiction to fossil fuels and nuclear energy. One of the fundamental reasons that giant urban areas and industries are unsustainable is because of their inherent dependency on huge quantities of dangerous and nonrenewable energy resources. To maintain a large, densely populated city requires immense quantities of coal, petroleum, or nuclear energy. It seems likely that safe and renewable energy sources such as wind, water, and solar power can probably not fully meet the needs of giant urban areas, even if careful energy conservation is practiced and automobile use and socially unnecessary production is curtailed. In contrast to coal, oil, and nuclear energy, solar, wind, and other alternative energy sources reach us mainly in small "packets," as it were. Yet while solar devices, wind turbines, and hydroelectric resources can probably not provide enough electricity to illuminate Manhattan Island today, such energy sources, pieced together in an organic energy pattern developed from the potentialities of a particular region, could amply meet the vital needs of small, decentralized cities and towns.

As with agriculture, the industrial economy must also be decentralized and its technology radically reworked to creatively utilize local resources in small-scale, multi-use facilities with production processes that reduce arduous toil, recycle raw materials, and eliminate pollution and toxic wastes. In this way, the *relatively* self-sufficient community, visibly dependent on its environment for its means of life, would likely gain a new respect for the organic interrelationships that sustain it. In the long run, the attempt to approximate local, or at least regional, self-sufficiency would prove more efficient than the wasteful and neo-colonial global division of labor that prevails today. Although there would doubtless be many duplications of small manufacturing and craft facilities from community to community, the familiarity of each group with its local environment and its ecological roots would make for a more intelligent and loving use of its environment.

Such a vision appears quite radical on the face of it. Yet I have to stress that my calls for decentralization and "alternative" technologies are, by themselves, insufficient to create a humane, ecological society. We should not delude ourselves into the belief that a mere change in demographics, logistics, design, or scale automatically yields a real change in social life or spiritual sensibility. Decentralization and a sophisticated alternative technology can help, of course. The kind of decentralized communities and eco-technologies that I've described here could help open up a new era of direct democracy by providing the free time and social comprehensibility that would make it possible for ordinary people to manage the affairs of society without the mediation of ruling classes, giant bureaucracies, or elitist professional political functionaries. However, a genuine ecological vision ultimately needs to directly answer such nagging questions as "who owns what?" and "who runs what?" The answers we give to these questions will have enormous power to shape our future.

I would argue that the best form of government in an ecological society would be direct democratic self-government; that the best form of ownership of productive enterprises and resources would be neither corporate nor state but communal at the municipal level; and that the best form of economic management would be community self-management. In such a vision, broad policies and concrete decisions that deal with community life, agriculture, and industrial production would be made, whenever possible, by active citizens in face-to-face assemblies. Among the many benefits of such a democratic, cooperative commonwealth is the fact that it would help encourage a non-hierarchical, non-domineering sensibility within the human community that would ultimately influence human society's view of its relationship with the rest of the natural world.

To be sure, moving from today's capitalist society—based on giant industrial and urban belts, a highly chemical agribusiness, centralized and bureaucratic power, a staggering armaments economy, massive pollution, and exploited labor—towards the ecological society that I have only begun to describe here will require a complex and difficult transition strategy. I have no pat formulas for making such a revolution. A few things seem clear, however. A new politics must be created that eschews the snares of co-optation within the system that is destroying social and ecological life. We need a social movement that can effectively resist and ultimately replace the nation-state and corporate capitalism; not one that limits its sights to "improving" the current system.

Direct nonviolent resistance is clearly an important element of this new politics. The marvelous genius of the anti-nuke alliances of the 1970s was that they intuitively sensed the need to break away from the "system" and form a strong independent opposition. To a large extent, to be sure, they adopted a direct-action strategy because earlier attempts to stop nuclear power plants by working within the system had failed. Endless months or years of litigation, hearings, the adoption of local ordinances, petitions, and letter writing campaigns to congresspeople had all essentially failed to stop the construction of new nuclear power plants. Stronger measures were required in order to finally stop new construction. Yet I believe that an even more important feature of direct action is that it forms a decisive step toward recovering the personal power over social life that the centralized, overbearing bureaucracies have usurped from the people. It provides an experiential bridge to a possible future society based on direct grassroots democracy.

Similarly, community organizing is a key element of a radical new politics, particularly those forms of association where people meet face-to-face, identify their common problems, and solve them through mutual aid and volunteer community service. Such community organizations encourage social solidarity, community self-reliance, and individual initiative. Community gardens, block clubs, land trusts, housing cooperatives, parent-run daycare centers, barter networks, alternative schools, consumer and producer cooperatives, community theaters, study groups, neighborhood newspapers, public access television stations—all of these meet immediate and usually neglected community needs. But, they also serve, to greater or lesser degrees, as schools for democratic citizenship. Through participation in such efforts we can become more socially responsible and more skilled at democratically discussing and deciding important social questions.

However—and this may shock most conventional anarchists—I also think we need to explore the possibilities of grassroots electoral politics. While it cannot be denied that most ways of participating in the electoral arena only serve to legitimize the nation-state, with its standing bureaucracy and limited citizen involvement, I think it is important and possible for grassroots activists to intervene in local politics and create *new* kinds of local structures such as ballot initiatives, community assemblies, town meetings, and neighborhood councils that can increasingly take over direct democratic control of municipal governments.

The success of such a libertarian municipalist movement will depend on its ability, over time, to democratize one community after another and establish confederal regional relationships between these local communities. We will need such a geographical, political, and economic base if we are ever to seriously challenge the nation-state and multinational corporations. We will need to create such a *dual power* in order to wrest important and immediate concessions from the existing system and ultimately to supplant it. I see no other realistic alternative for creating a genuinely ecological society.

Such a revolution will obviously not happen all at once in some grand, spontaneous, and violent insurrection. The new politics I advocate has an almost cellular form of growth, a process that involves organic proliferation and differentiation like that of a fetus in a womb. While an ecological revolution will require confrontational struggles, now and in the future, it will also require patient, long-term local community organizing and imaginative grassroots political work.

This strategy is what I mean by green politics. The goal here is not simply to "represent" the growing citizens' movement by taking over the existing top-down political apparatus of the municipality, let alone the nation-state. The goal is to establish or restore town meetings, neighborhood assemblies, or even neighborhood councils of active citizens as the foundation of local control. Radical ecology candidates should run in local elections on a platform fundamentally oriented toward establishing such citizen assemblies and legally restructuring the governance structure of the city by placing a premium on political participation, face-to-face discussion of the public's business, and the complete accountability of citizens who are elected delegates to larger, confederal councils or who serve on purely administrative bodies.

These neighborhood assemblies can also be started before they are legally recognized. Indeed, unofficial citizen assemblies could establish a "shadow" or "parallel" city council that is made up of elected and recallable delegates from each neighborhood assembly. Such shadow city councils, while legally powerless in their initial phases, could exercise a very effective *moral* influence on an official city council until they acquire increasing legal power of their own. They could track the agenda and business of the official city councils in close detail, propose needed reforms, and challenge any legislative measures that they find incompatible with the public interest, thereby mobilizing the people into an increasingly effective political force.

As direct political democracy is being institutionalized, piecemeal steps can also be taken on many different levels to increase the municipalization of the economy. While not infringing on the proprietary rights of small retail outlets, service establishments, artisan shops, small farms, local manufacturing enterprises, and homeowners, this new kind of municipality could start to purchase larger economic enterprises, particularly those enterprises that are about to be closed and could be managed more efficiently by their own workers than by profit-oriented entrepreneurs or corporations. The use of land trusts as a means not only for providing good public housing but promoting small-scale artisanal production could occupy a high place on the agenda of a municipality's economic program. Cooperatives, community gardens, and farmers' markets could be fostered with municipal funds and placed under growing public oversight—a policy that might very well command greater consumer loyalty than we would expect to find toward profit-oriented corporate enterprises.

In such a political and economic context, the ecological restoration of the municipality and the surrounding countryside could begin to take firm root. Public lands could be expanded and restored. Farmers could be supported to make the transition to diversified, organic forms of agriculture to meet local and regional needs. Corporate farms could be increasingly restricted. Programs could be started to facilitate the reconstruction and repopulation of rural areas by interested city dwellers willing to create new communities of their own. Safe and effective birth-control methods could be made available free or at low cost. Recycling could become mandatory. Local business and residential codes could encourage significant energy conservation and promote a switch over to safe and renewable energy sources. The shift to ecologically sound production technologies could begin.

Finally, we cannot hope to realize this vision in only one neighborhood, town, or city. Ours needs to be a confederal society based on the coordination of all municipalities in a bottom-up system of administration as distinguished from the top-down rule of the nation-state. Be it on a county-wide or regional basis, our new municipalities should be united by confederal councils, each occupied by popularly chosen "deputies" who are easily recallable by the communities they serve. These confederal bodies should be strictly *administrative;* they would make no *policy* decisions but merely coordinate and administer decisions made by the municipal citizens' bodies that select them.

Confederation, which has a long though almost lost history of its own, should not be confused with the state, which has always conflicted with confederal structures presumably in the name of "efficiency" and, very typically, the "complexity" of our "modern" society. These claims are sheer hogwash. What troubles me today is that so many radicals accept the claptrap about the "complexities" of modern society and rarely recognize that when cities have eight, ten, or twelve million residents they are no longer even "cities" but shapeless disempowered urban blobs that are direly in need of decentralization— physically as well as institutionally.

Of course, all these ideas about a left libertarian municipal strategy are only the bare outlines of a *minimal* program for moving towards social and ecological harmony. This strategic approach, however, would help solve a number of immediate problems and point us in the direction of more fundamental social changes. It would begin to build up a popular dual power base from which to effectively challenge the corporations and the nation-state. Successful alliances can likely be built around every element of this minimal program because its goals are rooted in a *general* human interest that transcends the real but particularistic interests of class, nationality, ethnicity, and gender. Such genuinely populist goals can be formulated in ways that can unite a majority of people—men and women, people of different colors, poor folks, workers in industrial and service industries, and middle-class professionals as well as a few of our elitist opponents who just might have their consciences pricked.

I do agree with Linda, however, on one crucial point. It will be an unpardonable failure in political creativity if a green movement that professes to speak for a new ecological politics in this country indulges in a "hate America" mood or thinks and speaks in a political language that is unrelentingly negative or incomprehensible to the majority of the American people. For decades, radicals have talked to the North American people in the language of German Marxism, Russian Leninism, Chinese Maoism, or, less frequently, Spanish anarchism—indeed, in virtually every language but one that stems from the American revolutionary tradition itself, with its empasis on community, decentralism, individuality, and direct democracy in oposition to the concentration of state and corporate power, imperialistic trade, and unbridled greed.

We need to consciously revive an older image of the "American Dream" that was communitarian, democratic, and utopian, however defective it was in other respects. While the current system is rotten at its core, it still retains vestiges of earlier, often more libertarian institutions that have been very uncomfortably incorporated into the present ones. Let's build on these institutions and traditions. To use a slogan I've coined in recent years, "We must democratize the republic and then radicalize the democracy."

Chapter 4

Racism and the Future
of the Movement

Jim Haughton:

I agree with Murray and Dave on their very strong and emphatic statement that this society is rotten to the core, but I must insist that it was rotten from its very inception. We cannot simply seek a return to an imagined libertarian, democratic past. While "the founding fathers" were talking about building a democracy in this country, they were also dragging people here from Africa as slaves and were decimating Native Americans who were resisting the European occupation. Obviously, the American conception of democracy was flawed right from the start. What has happened over the past three hundred years has been the perfecting of a society based, from its very beginning, on predatory behavior, a callous disregard for human life, and the mad search for profit.

This predatory behavior has also been directed, from the very start, at the ecological community as well. When Native Americans freely inhabited North America, there was a great respect for the land and its non-human inhabitants. This has been lost since the European invasion. Not long after the Europeans arrived here with their indentured servants, slaves, and their aristocracy, land became nothing more than real estate to be taken from tribal communities and divided up by white Europeans into private parcels and exploited for profit within an ever-expanding market. The wilderness was feared and hated by most white settlers. Wilderness, like the Indians, stood in the way of the maximum exploitation of the New World. They both had to be destroyed.

The modern environmental or ecology movement marks an important break with this corrupt worldview. I have a great respect for this movement. The ecological question is clearly the overriding ethical and survival question confronting the human race today. Yet, I wonder how profound a break with our nation's past the ecology movement can actually spark if it is unwilling to also confront the question of racism. Racism has been the foundation of the American social system. Our country is a racist system from top to bottom. Racism has become so integral to American life that people don't even see it or respond to it any longer.

To date, the ecology movement has reflected this history more often than it has broken with it. The movement has often one-sidedly challenged our society's destructiveness towards non-human nature but ignored its ongoing and direct degradation of human beings, particularly of poor people of color who are among the most victimized. The movement has all too often developed its program in ways that stand in conflict with the short- and long-term needs of poor people of color all over the world. Because of its history as a predominantly white and middle-class movement, the environmental movement's vision has been incomplete, and important alliances have not been made.

These neglected alliances may hold the key to the future of the struggle for an ecological society. To their credit, both Murray and Dave have clearly identified capitalism as one of the greatest sources of danger for the world of life. They are right. We do live in a society where there is a ruling class that owns or controls all the basic resources and institutions of society, where the very dynamics of the system require constant growth and exploitation, and where the general interest for grassroots democracy, human solidarity, and ecological balance is thwarted to meet the special interests of the ruling class. This raises the question, however, of how can we organize a broad-based movement that can fundamentally change this system.

What we need to understand is that one of the most important keys to the ruling class being able to divide and conquer and wield its power, at least in this country, is racism. Historically, racism has divided masses of ordinary Americans who are in reality natural and logical allies in the struggle against the destructive effects and under-lying elite institutions of corporate capitalism. Racism has thus been a strategic disaster for any social movement in this country aiming at reform or fundamental change. There is perhaps no force that has been more divisive. We have seen it wreck or limit movements over and over again in our history.

Can the ecology movement afford, either morally or strategically, to ignore racism and the importance of bridging the racial gap? Can it afford to concern itself only with wilderness areas and non-human life and ignore the degraded and unhealthy environments in the workplace, in our urban communities, and in our rural areas that disproportionately affect working-class people and poor people of color? Can it afford to lose potential allies because of its indifference or lack of knowledge?

My question to Dave and Murray is what ideas do either of you have for building alliances across racial lines that can foster a broad-based ecological movement strong enough to make fundamental change? How can the ecological movement move to expand its base, deepen its vision, and combat racism?

Dave Foreman:

First of all, it is not going to be easy. Racism runs deep within our national history. I see it in my own family history. My ancestry is entirely northern European. My family came to Calvert County, Maryland, in the early 1600s. They moved to the Shenandoah Valley. They followed Daniel Boone across the Wilderness Road into Kentucky displacing native tribal communities that had lived in the area for generations. For a while, my family had a plantation there and owned slaves. They fell on hard times though, like many cotton farmers who wore out their land, and they ultimately lost the plantation. Most of my family ended up poor hillbillies in Eastern Kentucky. I come from this American tradition that Jim has so eloquently criticized, a tradition that gives little thought to the ethics of exploiting the land or people of color. I remember visiting relatives of mine in San Antonio, Texas back in the 1950s when the bathrooms were still segregated. At the time, I didn't think anything about it. It was "natural." That was just the way it was. I'm a product of this deeply entrenched racist tradition in the United States. Like other white environmentalists, it undoubtedly affects my politics and organizing.

Yet I believe building alliances across racial lines can be done. For example, in Los Angeles, the local Earth First! group has been working with a predominantly black group in Watts organizing against a toxic incinerator being built in the neighborhood. Such a campaign is a little outside of Earth First!'s usual focus on wilderness and endangered species, but it is an issue which clearly links the struggle for racial justice with an unpolluted environment. L.A. Earth First! thought it would be a useful way to build a militant environmental alliance across racial lines.

Ecological problems such as polluting incinerators, dangerous land fills, and toxic industrial waste sites are a huge survival issue for communities of color throughout this country. Indeed, poor communities, with high percentages of people of color, are far more likely to be chosen as the sites of such environmental and public health hazards than white and more middle-class communities. Environmentalists and civil rights groups can make common cause around such issues and they should. The predominantly white and middle-class anti-nuke alliances of the 1970s never fully appreciated this possible linkage of issues when they organized their direct action campaigns against nuclear power plants. They would undoubtedly have been much stronger if they had put greater effort in building alliances across racial lines. The issue was there, only the needed coalition-building was missing.

Happily, a growing and militant, multiracial, grassroots "movement for environmental justice" is organizing around such issues in more and more poor communities across the United States.[1] Groups such as the Highlander Folk Center in Tennessee have been providing training and leadership development for this movement, paying particular attention to encouraging the leadership of community women and people of color. I am very encouraged by such organizing. While it is not Earth First!'s primary organizing focus, I am glad other groups are taking it on. That is as it should be. I strongly believe that the big mainstream environmental organizations should provide strong financial and logistical support for such struggles and that radical white ecologists would also do well to participate actively in such grassroots organizing.

I am convinced, however, that groups like Earth First! do not have to shift their focus away from their primary goal of protecting wilder-

ness areas and endangered species in order to build alliances across
racial lines. It would be a huge mistake to believe that such organizing
is irrelevant to communities of color. It may not seem like an obvious
survival issue to African-Americans who have been isolated in dena-
tured, rundown urban areas and who are trying desperately to keep
their heads above water and maintain their ravaged communities, yet
it is ultimately relevant to their lives. Protecting the rainforests is a
question of survival for the planet, including the human species.
Furthermore, while most African-Americans understandably have
more immediate survival concerns, the rainforests are home to many
indigenous tribal peoples and peasants who depend on the forests for
their physical and cultural survival and who find the forest community
inherently valuable and worthy of human respect.

   The international rainforest preservation movement has provided a wonderful cross fertilization between indigenous tribal peoples
and environmentalists in the United States, Japan, and Western Europe. This experience has deepened much of the U.S. ecology
movement's perspective. I personally have learned a great deal from
my interactions with these tribal peoples. I have come to strongly
appreciate the need for the ecology movement to directly join the fight
against imperialism and the continuing oppression of tribal peoples
throughout the world. While we need to fight to protect the forest, we
also need to fight to protect those tribal cultures which have historically
lived in harmony with the forests and respected them. I am proud of
the international support we have been able to muster for these people
and for the fact that several tribal groups are using my book *Ecodefense*
as a guide to fight logging and other forms of commercial encroachment
on the ecological integrity of their forest communities.

   I have long believed it is important to understand the racial
dynamic that underlies so much of the ecological crisis. We need to
clearly face up to the fact that white males from North America and
northern Europe hold a disproportionate share of responsibility for the
mess we're in; that upper- and middle-class consumers from the First
World take an excessive portion of the world's resources and therefore
cause greater per capita destruction than do other peoples.

   It is largely based on this understanding that the Earth First!
movement has developed such a great affinity with native groups
throughout the world. Overall, they are in the most direct and respect-

ful relationship with the natural world. Earth First! has therefore tried to back such groups in common struggle whenever we can. Most Earth First!ers, for example, are supportive of the Dine (Navajo) of Big Mountain in their struggle against the U.S. government's plan to forcefully relocate them. Several have been working hard on that.

I think white environmentalists should take on such struggles with much greater frequency and begin making important organizing connections to these communities and other people of color. However, one problem I have seen over and over again among a number of white organizers trying to build coalitions with people of color is that they get so caught up in their own white guilt that they put people of color on a pedestal and make them immune from questioning or criticism. This is a disaster for alliance-building. It short-circuits the learning process that needs to take place among all parties to an alliance.

I think it is right and important for Jim to criticize the residual racism in the ecology movement and to criticize the ecology movement when it only values struggles for wilderness preservation and ignores or disparages the environmental and survival struggles of poor people of color. We have much to learn from such criticism. We have made numerous mistakes that need to be corrected. However, I also think it is right and important for ecology groups to criticize communities of color if they develop their programs without sufficient thought or appreciation for the planet. If an alliance is to be meaningful, the critical questioning has to go both ways. It is true that we do need to be concerned about the oppression of women, of workers, of people of color. But we must also remember that members of other species are among the most oppressed beings on the planet.

Right now, we are waging an incredible war of genocide and domination against the natural world. So, while we should support the Dine people, we should not pretend that severe overgrazing by domesticated sheep does not occur on the Navajo reservation. While we support subsistence lifestyles by natives in Alaska wilderness, we should not be silent about clearcutting of old-growth forest in southeast Alaska by native corporations, or about the efforts of the Eskimo Doyon Corporation to push for oil exploration and development in the Arctic National Wildlife Refuge.

We do, however, need to be thoughtful and respectful in how we criticize and question each other. Alliance-building efforts can be destroyed as much by inappropriate criticism as they can by uncritical silence. Finding the creative middle ground is not often easy. I think Earth First! has sometimes failed to criticize our allies in the main-stream environmental movement productively.

The slogan of Earth First! is "No compromise in defense of Mother Earth." But what exactly does "no compromise" mean? It means waging confrontational struggles against ecocidal corporations and government agencies, of course. Yet too often when you fight regularly with powerful and intransigent institutions you can't get out of that mode of interaction when you are among actual or potential friends and discussing your differences. We often relate to our potential allies with the same strident, provocative, no-compromise attitude. This makes productive dialogue very difficult. We must guard against this. There are some real differences of opinion and differences of percep-tion among those active on various issues. These can't be wished away or ignored. Yet, we need to find an open, cooperative, and compromis-ing way of talking together and weaving our disparate struggles into a unified movement.

I think there was a mechanism in primal cultures for that. If you went out to hunt or to raid horses or to engage in a skirmish with another group of people, you went through certain rituals to prepare yourself for that. However, before you were reintegrated back into your own community you had to go through certain purification rituals to make sure you fully found your way back. That is something we have forgotten how to do. If we are really going to learn how to cooperate across racial, class, or experiential lines, we need to learn how to fight like hounds from hell against those institutions which threaten us all while at the same time we maintain a sense of community and connection among ourselves, even as we struggle to resolve our own differences. We need to recognize that these contradictions among ourselves are different from the contradictions between all of us and the guardians of the imperial status quo.

Establishing such guidelines on how to approach critical discus-sions across racial lines is purely academic, however, unless people are in actual contact with each other and talking together. Without actual contact, we simply will not realize how we're part of the same struggle and that we ultimately need each other. How we get there from here, how we overcome past divisions, and how we make connections is a very difficult question. I've already given some examples of how the ecology movement can make such alliances through common, coalition struggles. These efforts should be expanded, but I think environmentalists need to push themselves at a more personal level as well.

Building bridges among communities and movements also has a very personal and individual dimension to it. We need to seek out chances to learn about each other's lives, interests, and concerns. While I was in federal custody, after I got busted by the FBI, I met a number of people in jail that I ordinarily would not have come across in my daily life. Since I had been on TV, I was sort of a celebrity prisoner. Everybody wanted to take me under their wing and show me around. While in jail, I met a number of illegal aliens and heard many stories about the border patrol and living along the U.S.-Mexico border. It was conversations like these that helped me understand how the border patrol and the so-called drug war are part of an effort to create the apparatus and public acceptance for a racist police state in this country. Such conversations have significantly expanded my political concerns and perspectives.

Environmentalists also have much to contribute to the perspectives of many poor communities of color which have been forcibly divested of their direct connections with the land and isolated in decaying urban environments. I think that Outward Bound and other groups like it have done some good work setting up programs to get inner-city people of all ethnic backgrounds out into the wilderness in order to enrich their lives and expand their appreciation of the wild world. I have taken my sister's in-laws, who are working-class Hispanics, on raft trips through the river canyons of northern New Mexico to try to make the same connection. My nephew has become a wildlife fanatic. He probably has the longest life list of birds of any kid in New Mexico. I've also been talking about all of this with Bunyon Bryant, who is possibly the only black professor of natural resources in the country. We are currently planning a raft trip to bring together a select group of people to talk about how to work together to help restore and deepen the lost ecological awareness of so much of the urbanized African-American community.

Ultimately, however, I have no firm and final answers to Jim's questions. These are just some initial thoughts in a complex process.

It will likely take a few generations of hard work, at least, to thoroughly overcome the social wounds that divide us and inhibit our full cooperation. I don't think forming a large, all-encompassing movement organization that aims at effectively addressing all of our issues is practical or wise right now. I think any attempt along these lines will collapse of its own weight. What I think we need now is a greater effort to cooperate and learn from each other as well as a greater acceptance for the diversity of our primary interests and emphases. This seems to me the best framework for cooperation and alliance-building right now.

Perhaps a good analogy for what we need today would be the hunter/gatherer tribe which often splits into small family bands of just a few people and then, a few times a year, comes together as a larger group for socialization and exchanging ideas, experiences, and, how should I say it, genetic material. I think we need to view the larger movement as an increasingly powerful river with many currents in it. Sometimes those currents may flow separately; sometimes they are going to directly merge and flow together. All of these currents, however, are still part of the same river. The trick is to make sure all these currents flow in the same direction. Let's face it, there is a big ugly dam downstream that we need to topple over and break apart. We are going to need to cooperate if we are going to be strong enough to do that. We need to make the effort to build alliances now.

In closing, let me just quote Henry David Thoreau, "Let your life be a counter-friction to stop the machine."[2]

Murray Bookchin:

I am moved by Jim's and Dave's remarks. One of my major complaints about "deep ecology" is that it lacks a clearly developed social analysis and ethics. It thus provides a "tolerant" philosophical home to profoundly conflicting ideas and sensibilities, from humanistic naturalists in the tradition of Thoreau to barely-disguised racists. Today, Dave seems to be standing with the former. I welcome this after some of the misanthropic and neo-Malthusian articles I've encountered in *Earth First!* in the recent past.

Over the years, some of the most visible spokespeople of Earth First! have clearly fallen into the latter category. Slogans like "Rednecks for Wilderness" are, at the very least, insensitive and unlikely to build bridges across racial differences. Such a slogan is charged with racist overtones for African-Americans. More dangerous still have been the published statements by prominent deep ecologists associated with Earth First! calling AIDS—which has been particularly devastating in the black and gay communities—an environmentalist's dream come true, or dealing with famines in Ethiopia as a sad but presumably necessary means of controlling Third World population, or viewing Latin American Hispanics as "culturally-morally-generically" inferior people who should be barred from emigrating to the United States and using up "our" resources.

The problem, of course, is not deep ecology's stated commitment to foster a new sensibility towards the natural world. All radical ecologists agree on the need to go beyond the limited environmentalist perspective that sees "Nature" as merely a passive inventory of "natural resources" and defines appropriate human interaction with the natural world as merely using these resources "efficiently" and "prudently" without threatening the biological "sustainability" of the *human* species. Whatever our differences about nature philosophy, both deep and social ecologists call for a direct and profound respect for the biosphere, a conscious effort to function within its parameters, and an attempt to achieve harmony between society and the natural world. I believe that all social activists should embrace this new sensibility towards nature.

The main problem with deep ecology's philosophy, however, is that this is about as far as it goes. It does not highlight or systematically address the *social* roots of the ecological crisis. It does not document or interpret the historical emergence of society out of first, or biological, nature, a crucial development that brings social theory into organic contact with ecological theory. It presents no explanation of—indeed, it reveals little interest in—the emergence of hierarchy out of early organic society, of classes out of hierarchy, of the state out of classes—in short, the highly graded social as well as ideological developments which are at the roots of the ecological problem. Indeed, it is hardly more insightful about these questions than the reformist environmental movement. Thus, even when individual deep ecologists show concern for harmonizing relationships between races, genders, and classes, their concern does not stem from a coherent expression of deep ecology philosophy. Rather it is expressed only as an external ethical and social commitment that may—or may not, for that matter—be added to a deep ecology perspective.

Women, poor folks, and people of color are right, I think, to be very wary of a philosophy which interprets vital questions of human solidarity, democracy, and liberation as optional and secondary concerns, at best, and evidence of "anti-ecological" or "anthropocentric" selfishness, at worst. Ecological philosophy, if it is to provide a solid basis for alliance-building, must be a *social* ecology that critiques and challenges *all* forms of hierarchy and domination, not just our civilization's attempt to dominate and plunder the natural world. It must set as its overarching goal, the creation of a non-hierarchical *society* if we are to live in harmony with nature.

Our present society has a definite hierarchical character. It is a propertied society that concentrates economic power in corporate elites. It is a bureaucratic and militaristic society that concentrates political and military power in centralized state institutions. It is a patriarchal society that allocates authority to men in varying degrees. And *it is a racist society* that places a minority of whites in a self-deceptive sovereignty over a vast worldwide majority of peoples of color. While it is theoretically possible that a hierarchical society can biologically sustain itself, at least for a time, through draconian environmentalist controls, it is absolutely inconceivable that present-day hierarchical and particularly capitalist society could establish a non-domineering and ethically symbiotic relationship between itself and the natural world. As long as hierarchy persists, as long as domination organizes humanity around a system of elites, the project of dominating nature will remain a predominant ideology and inevitably lead our planet to the brink, if not into the abyss, of ecological extinction.

Social ecology provides a better foundation for alliance-building and a respectful unity-in-diversity because it understands that the very concept of dominating nature stems from the domination of human by human, indeed, of the young by their elders, of women by men, of one ethnic or racial group by another, of society by the state, of one economic class by another, and of colonized people by a colonial power. It thus stresses all the social issues that most deep ecologists and reform environmentalists tend to ignore, often downplay, or badly misunderstand. From this perspective, the fight against racism is not just a mere political item that can be added to "defending the Earth;"

it is actually a vital and essential part of establishing a truly free and ecological society. The difficult work of building alliances across ethnic lines is thus seen, as Jim so correctly says, as a moral as well as strategic imperative for the ecology movement.

I feel this moral imperative very deeply. Back in the early 1940s, I worked and served as a union steward in a foundry where over 80 percent of my fellow workers were black. As a result of this experience, I was able to see the lives of my African-American brothers in all their richness and their oppression. I experienced this again working in the civil rights movement during the late 1950s and early 1960s with the Congress of Racial Equality. Today, I feel I am witnessing not only racist exploitation. I am witnessing the very destruction of the black community. I see genocide at work against black people and other people of color throughout the cities of America. It horrifies me. Twenty-four percent of all black males in New Haven between the ages of twenty and thirty now have AIDS viruses. These people are not being helped; their fate is being "acknowledged" as just another statistic in the reports of the Public Health Service. The horror of racism today, which has dramatically intensified since I first confronted it in the 1930s and 1940s, violates every sense of justice I feel. The ecology movement must stand firmly against racism and actively participate in the struggle against it.

One of the chief obstacles to building alliances across ethnic lines manifests itself at the programmatic level. One of the truisms of the environmental movement is that our society has reached ecological limits to its overall growth at the global level. Environmentalists thus call for limits on economic expansion, population growth, and individual consumption. There is a great deal of validity to such demands. I have long argued that we must transform our bloated, urbanized, and rapacious society into a confederation of eco-communities that are sensitively tailored in size, population, technology, and consumption to the specific ecosystems in which they are located. But when these demands are not set clearly within the context of a struggle for a non-hierarchical society, appeals for "limits to growth" are almost inevitably turned into racist and draconian measures by the powers-that-be to ensure the sustainability of hierarchical First World societies at the expense of the material needs of Third World people. It should not come as a surprise, then, that for many activists of color environmentalism has come to mean little more than racist measures for blocking needed economic improvements and for intensifying austerity among people of color in this country and in Latin America, Asia, and Africa. It has also come to mean a vicious policy of limiting the "surplus" population of people of color throughout the world through starvation, disease, and forced sterilization.

It is bad enough when reform environmentalists are naively complicit with this perversion of valid ecological objectives. It is shocking to me, however, when self-identified deep ecologists actively embrace such measures and call their views "radical ecology." I may have seemed very disputatious in dealing harshly with these tendencies in the ecology movement but I think my zealousness is justified. Such views make productive alliances across ethnic lines nearly impossible. I cannot be "mellow" on this point. Both explicit and implicit racism must be challenged and uprooted from within our movement. To ignore this need is to court moral and strategic disaster.

Besides making the changes I've urged here in our ecological philosophy and the way we develop and articulate our program, I am convinced that the best way to build productive alliances across ethnic lines is for the radical ecology movement to adopt libertarian municipalism as one of its major strategies for change. We certainly need the direct action campaigns of Earth First! to defend wilderness areas. Yet, if we are really going to move towards an ecological society based on confederated, democratic communities—artfully tailored to our ecosystems—we also need to develop a new grassroots municipal politics.

As I said before, we need to develop our tactics of nonviolent direct action, community organizing, and local electoral politics into a strategy geared towards gaining direct democratic control of our communities and transforming them along the lines suggested in my response to Linda Davidoff. If we are to be effective, radical ecologists must try to create organic communities—organic no less in their respect for land, flora, and fauna than in their attempts to foster human solidarity, grassroots democracy, and social support systems.

We can already see the seeds for such a movement. I agree with Dave that local issues such as the siting of nuclear reactors or nuclear waste dumps, the dangers of acid rain, and the presence of toxic dumps, to cite only a few of the many problems that beleaguer innumerable American municipalities, have already united an astonishing variety of people into grassroots movements which transcend traditional class, ethnic, and social barriers that have historically divided our communities. I fully agree with Jim that vital coalitions between ecologists and people of color that challenge the state and corporations are quite possible at the local grassroots level.

Over the last few decades, demands for local community control have yielded a multitude of block associations, tenants' groups, alternative institutions, neighborhood alliances, and multiracial citizen action groups. The town meeting, or citizens assembly, initially a New England institution, is becoming a byword in regions of the United States that have no shared tradition with the Northeast. Community action groups have also begun to enter into local politics, a terrain that was once the exclusive preserve of elite party machines. They are doing this on a scale that is beginning to affect municipal policymaking.

Grassroots politics, specifically popular municipal politics, is becoming an integral part of U.S. politics as a whole. While it has yet to find a coherent voice and a clear sense of direction, I hope it is here to stay and will work its way, however confusedly, into the real world of the political landscape. Put bluntly, a latent *dual power* must emerge in which the local base of society begins to challenge the authority of its seemingly invulnerable state and corporate apex. I think we can develop such a tendency in North America today. I think it possible—if a highly conscious, well-organized, and programmatically coherent libertarian municipalist movement develops in the next decades—for the people to reconstruct society along lines that could foster a balanced, well-rounded, and harmonious community of interests among each other and between humanity and nature.

Such an approach is not a utopian dream; it is an urgently needed strategy for our own time. Because of automation, the flight of capital, and the emerging global division of labor, a number of U.S. cities and towns have been transformed in the eyes of corporate and government elites from sites for maintaining essential "human resources" into a dumping ground for superfluous "human waste." To varying degrees, cities like New York, Detroit, and St. Louis have been set adrift by the corporations and the state. They have been abandoned to their squalor and to a leprous process of decay. Not surprisingly, given our country's racist history, people of color comprise residential majorities in many of these cities. Owing to the decline of municipal services in these largely abandoned cities, a vacuum is developing between the traditional institutions that managed the city and the urban population itself. Understaffed and underfunded municipal agencies can no longer pretend to adequately meet such basic needs as sanitation, education, health, and public safety. An eerie municipal "no man's land" is emerging between the traditional, decaying institutional apparatus of these cities and the people it professes to serve.

As a result, many affluent city-dwellers have abandoned their communities. Many of the poor remain and are lost in despair, crime, violence, and drug addiction. Others, however, have become organizers and active citizens. These people are taking the first steps towards altering the social, political, economic, and natural landscape of their communities. They have stepped in to fill the void. Radical ecologists must support these active, civic-minded citizens and work closely with them.

While most social theorists still seem to lack a sufficient awareness of the public's power to create its own political institutions and forms of organization, there are many examples of that power that encourage me. One of my favorites is drawn from New York in the late 1970s. It was called the "East Eleventh Street Movement." Initially, the movement was a Puerto Rican neighborhood organization, one of several in the Lower East Side of Manhattan, which formed an alliance with some young ecologically-oriented radicals to rehabilitate an abandoned tenement that had been completely gutted by fire. The block itself, one of the worst in the Hispanic ghetto, had become a hangout for drug addicts, car-strippers, muggers, and arsonists. After being illegally taken over by community squatters, the building was totally rebuilt by co-opers, composed for the most part of Puerto Ricans, a few blacks, and some whites. The movement's attempts to acquire title to the building, to fund its rehabilitation, and expand its activities to other abandoned structures were to become a *cause célèbre* that inspired similar efforts both in the Lower East Side and other areas.

The building was taken over even before negotiations with the city had been completed. The city government was patently reluctant to assist the co-opers and had to be subjected to strong local pressure before supplying any aid. Ultimately, the building itself was not only rebuilt but was "ecologically retrofitted" with energy-saving devices, insulation, solar panels for heating water, and a wind generator to supply some of its electric power. There was talk of rooftop gardens, waste recycling, and turning abandoned lots nearby into neighborhood "vest-pocket" parks.

It would take too long to give a full account of the struggles of the East Eleventh Street Movement. Yet, I'm pleased to say that a number of people from the Institute for Social Ecology played a inspirational and technical role in these projects. Here, I think, is a little-known and remarkable example of how young white social ecologists worked hand-in-hand with oppressed Hispanic people to reclaim a human habitat in a truly ecological manner.

Perhaps the most significant feature of this struggle was its left-libertarian ambience. The rehab project was not only a fascinating structural enterprise; it was an extraordinary cooperative effort in every sense of the term. Politically, the Movement "fought City Hall" and it did so with an awareness that it was promoting decentralized neighborhood rights over the Big City machine. Economically, it fought the New York financial establishment by advancing a concept of labor— sweat equity—over the usual capital and monetary premises of investment. Ecologically, this movement experimented with eco-technologies, renewable energy sources, and relative independence from the giant utilities. Socially, it encouraged neighborhood pride, social solidarity, and community self-activity. It was a marvelous example of social ecology in action which contrasts markedly with the flighty, self-indulgent, and sometimes misanthropic features I often find in deep ecology and middle-class environmentalism.

From a desperate attempt to secure decent housing, a grassroots social ecology movement was born. Many other stories could be told about similar struggles in communities all over the country. That these grassroots movements are often ephemeral does not negate the existence of an underlying ferment and libertarian potential at the base of North American society. More importantly, for the purposes of this discussion, the existence of such movements suggests that successful multiracial alliances can be built around such social ecological efforts.

We need to be very careful in trying to build multicultural alliances, however. As I said earlier, one of the tasks of the radical ecology movement is to articulate a *general* human interest that transcends the real but particularistic interests of class, nationality, ethnicity, and gender in order to build alliances to reconstruct our communities along more humane and ecological lines. Yet we need to be wary of talking too glibly about the general human interest. Multiculturalism must mean more than mistaking the currently dominant culture as the universal and expecting other people to adopt the perspective of this dominant culture. This is not a productive trancendence of particularism. Unfortunately, such a narrow universalist perspective has historically plagued predominantly white and middle-class movements. It is thus all too easy for the ecology movement today to play fast and loose with concepts like "the people" and overlook particular class, ethnic, and gender interests that need to be forthrightly addressed within the larger context of a general human and planetary interest.

Jim Haughton is right in saying that such unresolved divisions among the people not only violate basic principles of social ethics but will also decrease the likelihood of our creating a genuinely ecological society. To avoid this, radical ecologists, whatever their backgrounds, need to remain in close solidarity with the specific liberation struggles of people of color, women, children, gays and lesbians, working people, the jobless poor, and colonized peoples. While deep ecologists have rarely emphasized this, these coalitions are part of the needed social struggles against the age-old traditions and institutions of hierarchy and domination—traditions that have warped society for thousands of years and have destructively shaped humanity's attitude toward the natural world. Let's not be a party to this neglect any longer. If we are really committed to creating an ecological society, we need to strive to make our lives a counter-friction to racism and all forms of domination and exploitation. This is an essential part of any genuinely radical ecological politics.

Part II

Closing Essays—One Year Later

Chapter 5

Second Thoughts
of an Eco-Warrior

Dave Foreman

As an activist, my chosen task is to argue the case of non-human nature. I resolutely stand with John Muir on the side of the bears in the war industrial society has declared against the Earth. Yet this does not mean that I hate human beings. It does not follow that I am unmoved by human suffering, economic injustice, imperialism, or abuses of human rights. While it is true that I don't identify myself as a leftist, for all the reasons I have mentioned, I do agree with much of the libertarian, democratic left on a large number of social concerns. I certainly recognize the need for increasing the connections between the left's social concerns and my heartfelt and longtime ecological concerns.

I have learned much from Murray Bookchin's criticisms and I acknowledge failings on my part in the past. I have often left unstated, and sometimes unexamined, the social components of problems like overpopulation, poverty, and famine while trying to discuss their biological nature. I have also not always made it clear that I abhor the human misery involved in such problems. I have been insensitive, albeit unintentionally, and for that I humbly apologize.

Let me give just two examples. In 1986, Professor Bill Devall, co-author of *Deep Ecology,* interviewed me for the Australian magazine *Simple Living.* In that interview I made two statements I now regret, one on famine in Ethiopia and the other on Latin American immigration to the United States. In the first example, I said, as part of a much

longer discussion of famine and overpopulation, that "the worst thing
we could do in Ethiopia is to give aid—the best thing would be to just
let nature seek its own balance, to let the people there just starve…the
alternative is that you go in and save these half-dead children who
never will live a whole life. Their development will be stunted. And
what's going to happen in ten years' time is that twice as many people
will suffer and die." On the question of immigration, I commented that
"letting the USA be an overflow valve for problems in Latin America
is not solving a thing. It's just putting more pressure on the resources
we have in the USA."[1]

While I think it is unfortunate that these two passing comments
have been used to deny the validity of everything I have to say and to
paint me as a racist and fascist clone of David Duke, I do agree that
these comments were both insensitive and simplistic. Taken out of the
context of my larger concerns and writings, I can see how these remarks
suggest a callous Fortress America chauvinism on my part. However,
in the first case, I did not clearly say what I really meant and, in the
second, I now reject some of what I did mean at the time.

Indeed, after listening carefully to the criticism I've received, I
have rethought and modified my opinion on illegal immigration. While
I still believe that massive and unlimited immigration into any country
is a serious problem, I do not support beefing up the Border Patrol and
the other agencies that try to keep Latin Americans out of this country.
I do not think that this is a realistic or ethical response to the underlying
problem.

As I said earlier, I have long been in deep sympathy with the
sanctuary movement. I have also always opposed the Reagan-Bush
effort to support the home-grown *caballero juntas* to the south and to
overthrow progressive reform governments like the Sandinistas in
Nicaragua. Indeed, I have long supported the U.S. solidarity
movement's attempt to aid and abet reform and revolutionary movements in Central America. I think we need to disband the CIA and
prohibit other U.S. government agencies from covert or overt military
intervention in the Third World. I am convinced that there will be no
land reform, no democracy, and no end to repression and death squads
without the Latin American middle class, rural *campesinos,* and urban
intellectuals uniting in disgust and effecting true reform through
revolutions such as that which toppled Somoza in Nicaragua.

Nonetheless, I still have honest questions about whether, by sticking to the liberal dogma about unlimited immigration, we might actually be postponing revolutions or effective democratic reform movements in Latin America. This is one of the potential costs of having our nation serve as an overflow valve for Latin America's unruly, angry, economically dispossessed, and politically active citizens, to say nothing of the ecological impact. While Ed Abbey's proposal to send every illegal refugee that is caught home with a rifle and a thousand rounds of ammunition may be considered flippant and impractical, its underlying spirit has some merit that liberals and far too many leftists ignore.

So while I apologize for how my views on illegal immigration may have been stated in the *Simple Living* interview, I cannot rid myself of my nagging questions about unlimited immigration. Despite all my sympathies and affections for the oppressed people of Mexico and Central America, despite my distaste for artificial national borders, despite my antipathy for the Border Patrol, I cannot convince myself that unlimited immigration from Latin America, or from anywhere else for that matter, will fundamentally solve problems either here or there. A little troll in the back of my brain keeps whispering nagging questions. Who is really being helped by unlimited immigration? Is it sustainable? Does it actually exacerbate social and ecological problems here and in Latin America? What are effective and humane solutions for the real and underlying problems in this tragic situation?

Similarly, I have serious doubts and nagging questions about conventional "humanitarian" foreign aid responses to the increasing problem of famine in the Third World. That is what I was trying to get at in my comments on famine in Ethiopia. In my oft-quoted remark about famine in Ethiopia, however, I failed to clearly make this point. Indeed, I implied through my sloppy, off-the-cuff remark that famine was *purely* a biological question of too many people and too few resources, completely unrelated to social organization, economic exploitation, or international relations. I also implied that the *best* possible social response was for us to do nothing, offer no assistance of any kind, and to just let the hungry starve. I very much regret the way I phrased these comments. Standing by themselves, out of context, they sound truly cold hearted.

The point I was trying to make, and which I think is made when the rest of the interview is taken into account, is that oftentimes a feel-good humanitarian response from the United States or Western Europe may not have the result we hope and may even have the opposite result. The problem of famine has a number of important causes which can and should be addressed by insightful, creative actions on the part of social movements in the United States and by the rest of the First World. There is undoubtedly a positive role that we can play even though the answers are not often clear to me and the problem is very complex and entrenched.

I still have honest questions about the much-admired relief effort during the Ethiopian famine of the mid-1980s. I think these questions desperately need to be explored. Did shipping food to Ethiopia actually alleviate suffering? Does such aid, at its best, ever do more than stave off abject starvation for a short time, while leaving the underlying problems untouched? What is the lot of those poor wretches kept alive by the food shipments in 1985-86? Did most survive with their bodies and minds intact or are they permanently disabled or handicapped? If the latter, will these unfortunates be an impossible burden preventing Ethiopia from dealing with its problems? These are terrible and hard questions I know, but I think we have to at least consider them given that another famine lurks on the horizon of that increasingly desert-like land.

We need to carefully analyze the on-the-ground results of this very sincere—and sometimes heroic—relief effort. From what I have read, it appears that very little was accomplished and that the Ethiopian military junta used the food supplies as a political weapon to favor those who supported the central government and to punish those who supported the rebels in the civil war. Is it implausible then to argue that the principal beneficiaries of the Ethiopian relief effort (besides the military junta) were the contributors to it in the West, who derived liberal, do-gooder satisfaction without having to confront the massive inequities between the First and Third Worlds or question the economic imperialism of transnational corporations and financial institutions like the World Bank or change their own excessively consumptive lifestyles?

I think it can be persuasively argued that such uncritical, one-shot relief efforts actually inhibit a well thought out, long-term aid program to help native agriculturalists get back on their feet with tools and crops suitable for their particular ecological conditions and social needs. Indeed, it has to be asked, and I admit it is a terrible question, if such last-minute relief efforts actually allow a human population stretched beyond the land's carrying capacity to eke out existence for a few more years and, in the process, cause even greater deterioration of the land's capacity to support humans and other species. There is that little troll in the back of my brain again. Do such liberal, humanitarian relief efforts do more harm than good in terms of both human beings and the land?

Certainly, a growing number of radical social activists are aware of many of the problems I raise here. Unfortunately, however, many leftists (and rightists) still posit simplistic reasons for the tragedy in places like Ethiopia due to their desire to make the strongest possible case for the particular institutional demon highlighted by their particular social ideology. They also frequently discount the ecological or biological factors that often underlie problems of famine.

Please, let's be realistic and admit that there are several different and interrelated demons at work fostering famine conditions and that overpopulation is one of them and has to be vigorously addressed. While I agree that the population question can be approached in narrow, racist, and fascistic ways, I strenuously reject the idea that any and all ecologically-grounded concerns about human overpopulation are racist and fascist. Is it racist and fascist, for example, to propose making birth control methods and devices, including the French abortion pill and sterilization, freely available to any woman or man in the world who desires them?

I am unwilling to silence the heretical troll in my brain in order to be certified "politically correct" by conventional leftists. Yet I do see the problem of overpopulation more clearly now than I did back in 1986. I have come to understand through Murray that those of us who worry about the results of the population bomb need to make our case as carefully as possible. We need to acknowledge the many social, cultural, and economic causes of population growth as well as the biological, and we need to campaign for economic justice and an end to maldistribution of land, food, and other necessities of life as well as for the humane and long-term reduction of the human population. That's my position on population. If anyone has a bone to pick with it, fine, but please criticize it and not some five-year-old, off-the-cuff, out-of-context statement that does not accurately represent my considered opinion.

Unfortunately, I doubt that these careful clarifications and apologies will satisfy all of my critics. There seems to be a dogmatic, blind rage among many of my critics that renders them incapable of entering into a reasoned dialogue with me to explore our various positions and political differences together. Murray is an appreciated exception. Sadly, those who shout me down at speaking engagements, loudly chanting "racist" or "fascist" at me, or who make the same vocal charges over and over again in the press, have made a straw man out of me that resembles their fantasies and fears far more than it resembles me or my positions. Even more sadly, I believe these angry and uninformed hecklers are playing into the hands of FBI provocateurs. The FBI has clearly targeted me and hopes to shut me up—not just through harassment with a phony felony indictment but by using their talents at movement disruption (honed during the COINTELPRO era against the Black Panthers, Martin Luther King, Jr., and the American Indian Movement) to exploit this straw man and label me a racist.[2]

I have frequently been written off completely by people whose sole knowledge of my political perspective is gleaned from these two short quotes of mine taken out of context from the vast amount I have said or written. I have also routinely been misquoted. And, perhaps most maddening of all, I have been smeared by "guilt by association." Unfortunately, it is commonly assumed by many of my critics that, because I admired Ed Abbey and was a longtime friend of his, I agree with every one of his opinions on every single topic that he ever chose to talk or write about. I have also been held responsible for every statement made in *Earth First!* while I was its editor. Personally, I would like to meet any editor of a movement publication who has always agreed with every word of every article that he or she has ever agreed to publish. This kind of guilt by association is simply absurd.

I am aware, however, that my personal brand of deep ecology politics does represent a real heresy from some of the orthodoxies embedded within most liberal and left opinion today. The little troll in the back of my mind frequently troubles me, too. Why shouldn't the difficult questions it raises trouble others? Perhaps one of my biggest differences with Murray is that I am significantly more pessimistic about the future than he. I am not sure we really have enough time to turn things around before most of the world is overtaken by famine, genocide, war, totalitarianism, plagues, and economic collapse. When I look into the future, it is rare that I see pretty scenes of protected wilderness, prosperous farms, soft-technology abundance, and smiling children. I hope for this. I work for it, but it usually seems like a long shot to me.

I value my heretical little troll, however, because if we do have any real hope to turn things around it will depend on squarely facing our predicament. There is no realistic hope until enough of us have the courage to correctly identify the root problems of the ecological crisis. These root problems most certainly include social, political, and economic aspects but they also include ecological and biological realities as well. We need to rethink and rebuild our social ethics and politics along ecological lines. That's where my little troll comes in handy. Facing up to the ecological roots of our predicament means, in large part, asking difficult and troubling questions about the limited carrying capacity of the Earth's biosphere.

This line of questioning is hard for people who have embraced the cornucopian myths of modern industrialism and the unending, historic march of material progress. It is particularly hard for liberals and leftists, many of whom believe that the only way to successfully overcome poverty and injustice is to exponentially expand the available economic surplus until we create a super-abundant, post-scarcity society where there is little need to fight over the size of everybody's slice of the economic pie because the pie itself is so huge. The very concept of ecological scarcity and carrying capacity limits calls this whole "utopian" project into question.

Interestingly, the basic ecological notion of carrying capacity is accepted when applied to cattle or elephants by all except the most beef-witted rancher or the most starry-eyed animal lover. Yet, we are loath to admit that we humans are animals, too, and that carrying capacity thus applies to us in some very real ways. My repeated statements about the reality of ecological scarcity may be the most heretical thing I have to say. It may indeed be the great divide between my view and that of most of my critics on the left (and the right). Any such suggestion is immediately called Malthusian and dismissed as long discredited, pseudo-scientific hog wash at best, and racist and imperialist propaganda at worst.

Thomas Malthus is, of course, an easy target for dismissal. His dire warnings of economic collapse and global famine in the early 19th century did not materialize as predicted. His argument that human population naturally grows at an exponential rate while food production only grows arithmetically was also simplistic. To his credit, however, Malthus was right about his general argument that human societies exist within an ecological context that presents real natural limits that human beings must either adapt to or ultimately suffer some form of social and ecological crash. The nature of our ecosystem provides many opportunities for the human species but it also presents human societies with serious biological constraints that are not of our own choosing and which can only temporarily be ignored.

Unfortunately, to deny this ecological reality leaves completely unchallenged the very social trends that are pushing our society to catastrophically overshoot the Earth's limited carrying capacity. Such ostrich-like ignorance will lead most likely, along with other social forces, to a hellish future fraught everywhere with famine, plagues, economic collapse, devastating war, genocide, and totalitarianism. To the extent that the social justice movement ignores the whole question of our overshooting the Earth's carrying capacity, it inadvertently contributes to the likelihood of this future for everyone.

Indeed, Malthus might be considered an optimist by the standards of the late 20th century, for he only focused on the constraints that limited food supplies posed for human population growth and economic development. As ecologically-minded political scientist William Ophuls points out,

> Instead of simple Malthusian overpopulation and famine, we must now also worry about shortages of the vast array of energy and mineral resources necessary to keep the engines of industrial production running, about pollution and other limits of tolerance in natural systems, about such physical constraints as the laws of thermodynamics, about complex problems of planning and administration, and about a host of other factors Malthus never dreamed of.[3]

I strongly recommend that every environmental and social justice activist read and grapple with William Catton's *Overshoot: The Ecological Basis of Revolutionary Change.* In his book, Catton provides the best and most informed discussion yet published on the relationship of carrying capacity to human societies. He restates Malthus' dictum in ecological terms as "The biotic potential of any species exceeds the carrying capacity of its habitat."[4] Human beings are included here just as are elephants or lemmings. This book might well change how you think about the world. I agree with Native American scholar Vine Deloria, Jr. who, on the back cover of Catton's book, describes it as "one of the most important books I have read in my lifetime."

By itself, however, Catton's instrumental evaluation of how to live successfully within the carrying capacity limits of the biosphere is not sufficient. There are several possible ways of life that do not, on a global level, overshoot the Earth's carrying capacity. Some of these ways are moral and benefit the entire community and others do not. A barely sustainable "resource-fascism" is more than a speculative possibility for the future. It may well be the path of least resistance. We thus need a strong ethical foundation in order to choose what kind of ecologically sustainable society we should work toward. We need, ultimately, to get clear on more than just the ecological carrying capacity constraints on our behavior. We also need to explore the ethical limitations we should adopt, in Aldo Leopold's words, on our "freedom of action in the struggle for existence."[5]

The libertarian left has some very good things to say about the ethical limitations on our behavior when it comes to the social relationships between members of the human community. Humanist social ethics foster a vision of society that is equitable, democratic, and respectful to all members of the human community. I myself subscribe to much of this ethical vision—as far as it goes. However, it is very limited. Unfortunately, the vast majority of the left, even the environmentally oriented left, has next to nothing to say about environmental ethics beyond an ultimately anthropocentric commitment to provide a sustainable, non-toxic, and aesthetically pleasing environment for all human beings.

To me, this leftist anthropocentrism represents a huge failure of moral imagination and will ultimately lead, if successful, to a world where Big Wilderness and a significant degree of biodiversity are lost forever. Everything inside me rebels against this callous, morally impoverished view. I believe a grizzly bear snuffling along Pelican Creek in Yellowstone National Park with her two cubs has just as much natural right to her life as any human has to his or hers. All living things have intrinsic value, inherent worth. Their value is not determined by what they will ring up on the cash register of the GNP, nor by whether or not they are aesthetically pleasing to human beings. They just are. They have traveled that same three-and-a-half-billion-year evolutionary course we have. They live for themselves, for their own sakes, regardless of any real or imagined value to human civilization. They should never be considered mere means to our ends for they are, like us, also ends in themselves.

If I were to suggest only one book for people to read on environmental ethics, it would be Aldo Leopold's *A Sand County Almanac*. Aldo Leopold perhaps thought harder about nature and our relationship to it than anyone else in 20th century America. Forest supervisor, game manager, pioneer ecologist, and university professor, Leopold was always on the cutting edge of conservation. His posthumously published *Almanac* ranks among the finest discussions of environmental ethics ever written. In fact, for my money, it is the most important, the loveliest, the wisest book ever penned. He has made thousands of people into heretics and frankly the times call for a generous dose of radical ecological heresy.

I believe that the intrinsic value of living things demands direct moral consideration in how we organize our societies. I reject anthropocentrism completely and argue that besides our social commitments we also need to honor direct moral duties to the larger ecological community to which we belong. We have a moral obligation to preserve wilderness and biodiversity, to develop a respectful and symbiotic relationship with that portion of the biosphere that we do inhabit, and to cause no unnecessary harm to non-human life. Furthermore, I believe that these moral obligations frequently supercede the self-interests of humanity. Human well-being is vitally important to me, but it is not the ultimate ethical value. I agree with Aldo Leopold that ultimately "a thing is right when it tends to enhance the integrity, stability, and beauty of the biotic community."[6] For social ethics to be ecologically grounded they must become consistent with this larger ecological moral imperative. That is why I am for Earth first.

Such an ecological sensibility is surely radical but it is far from new. It has been, in one form or another, a common feature of the philosophical outlook of most primal peoples throughout history. It has, however, just begun to gain significant ground among citizens of the industrialized nations. For many, it is a shocking departure from what they were brought up to believe. Right now, the whole field of environmental ethics is exploding as more and more people try to flesh out an almost intuitive non-anthropocentric orientation into a well-reasoned, usable ethic to guide human interaction with the rest of the natural world.

I dub my tentative attempts biocentrism, others like Warwick Fox describe their approach as ecocentrism. Murray Bookchin describes his approach as "the ethics of complementarity. There is, of course, much overlap between these various non-anthropocentric perspectives. There are also some serious disagreements about what constitutes a morally appropriate relationship between humanity and the rest of the natural world that deserve further discussion. Indeed, there are significant differences even among those who call themselves biocentrics. Philosopher Paul Taylor, for example, has written an elaborate treatise on the biocentric outlook on nature and, while I appreciate his effort, I take exception to much of his approach.[7] Biocentrism is hardly a monolithic perspective. Clearly, the search for Earth wisdom has just begun for most of us.

Arne Naess has noted that there are three fairly distinct tendencies within the deep, long-range, ecology movement: the "naturals," the "spirituals," and the "socials."[8] I am by temperament a "natural." My primary concern is conservation biology and the defense of the wild. However, politically, I have been drawn over time into an increasing appreciation of the "socials" who focus primarily on fundamentally reconstructing human society along socially and ecologically non-hierarchical lines. Such an approach is surely needed if we are to resolve the overarching ecological crisis which is shaking our planet. On my best days, I seek a creative synthesis of all of these approaches into an integrated and coherent perspective which can guide our movement even as radical ecology activists continue to specialize in their particular areas of interest. That is why I am proud to have taken part in this dialogue with Murray Bookchin, one of the pioneers of social ecology.

My fear, however, is that this synthesis will not ultimately take firm root and that one of these three tendencies will simply become so dominant that the vital contributions of the other perspectives will be minimized or lost. This concerns me because I believe it would weaken the larger movement even more than our current fractured condition, where all of the limited approaches are at least alive and well. I thus think that the most responsible stance for anyone in any of these tendencies is to assume that their approach is both valid and limited.

We need to be open to the criticisms of others in order to sharpen our own perspectives. We also need to be willing to sharpen the perspective of other wings of the movement through adding our own constructive criticisms to the ongoing dialogue and debate. And we must be tolerant and respectful of individuals with whom we may differ in this discussion. How can we create a human society that is tolerant and respectful of individuals if we cannot create a movement in which we are tolerant and respectful of individuals with whom we disagree?

My biggest worry about the limited perspective of a socially-oriented ecology is that it can all too easily become overwhelmingly social and insufficiently ecological. I see this tendency among many social ecologists when they argue that we should "work to reharmonize humanity with nature by reharmonizing the social relationships between human and human."[9] This strategic axiom appears to emphasize the traditional social concerns of the libertarian left over direct day-to-day struggles to defend wilderness, foster an ecological sensibility, or reconstruct our society's interaction with the rest of the natural world here and now. The view here seems to be that, once the social relationships between human beings are all resolved, an ecological sensibility will automaticly flower, and appropriate ecological changes in our society's relationship to nature will be made.

Certainly, not all social ecologists are under this illusion that our ecological problems can all wait to be resolved until after a libertarian, democratic social revolution is successful. Many, if not most, clearly realize that we don't have this luxury even if we want it. To his credit, Murray has explicitly and repeatedly expressed the need for organizing around both social and ecological questions in the here and now. Yet the way this social ecology slogan is formulated and frequently repeated by a variety of social ecology groups does suggest a subtle tendency among many socially-oriented ecologists to devalue the validity of the important (though admittedly limited) activities of the "naturals." Indeed, I suspect it represents a holdover from the anthropocentric perspective that is still so common among leftists and social justice activists.

Ironically, such a tendency can even be seen today within Earth First!, once a stronghold of non-anthropocentric "naturals." I have become increasingly uncomfortable with the influx of new people into Earth First! who seem more adapted to a traditional social and economic justice worldview than to a radical ecological one. These new activists seem to be drawn to the organization primarily because of its media exposure and our reputation for confrontational, kick-ass direct action. Frankly, I worry that rather than reflecting a process of creative synthesis, this evolution represents a subtle but increasing disregard for the valid insights of the early "naturals" who originally built Earth First!.

Mind you, these differences between the "old" and "new guard" in Earth First! are, for the most part, honest differences between decent people who respect one another. Furthermore, I feel that much vital and important work remains to be done by the most recent incarnation of Earth First!. Yet, given my perspective as an uncompromising, wilderness-loving "natural," I feel the need to work within a new organization explicitly committed to biocentrism and doggedly focused on ecological wilderness identification, preservation, and restoration. For this reason, I've left Earth First! and begun to explore with others the possibilities of starting a new organization along these lines. Hopefully, this new organization will complement the work of the many and varied groups in the conservation movement as well as provide a continuing clear voice for the "naturals" within the larger radical ecology movement as we all labor together to find a common, integrated perspective that overcomes the limitations of each radical ecological tendency while maintaining the vital insights of each.

Chapter 6

Where I Stand Now

Murray Bookchin

A year has passed since Dave Foreman and I discussed the problems and future of the ecology movement in a large New York auditorium—along with Paul McIsaac, Linda Davidoff, and Jim Haughton. I have seen no reason over this year to alter any of the views I expressed back then. Dave is still under indictment for what I believe are charges trumped up by the FBI to harass the radical ecology movement. He has my strongest support in his efforts to defend his civil rights—and to prevent the government and corporate interests from tarnishing the environmental movement as "terrorist." Further-more, over the course of this dialogue, I have come to respect Dave as a conservation activist and a human being. In the course of our dialogue, Dave and I have found some common ground.

Important political differences still exist, however, as Dave him-self readily admits. For example, in the past year, Earth First!'s northern California groups, and possibly others as well, appear to have veered toward a degree of social activism and perspective that is far more consistent with social ecology than with a deep ecology perspective, even as amended recently by Dave. As Redwood Summer organizer Judi Bari points out, Earth First! is no longer "just a conservation movement, it is also a social change movement."[1] I applaud the general direction of this ideological shift. Dave, however, has since left the Earth First! movement to start a more narrowly focused wilderness conservation organization. There is a political difference here.

My regret about the Earth First! movement, which I have admired from its very inception, is that so many of its activists do not openly

121

acknowledge that this *de facto* ideological shift has occurred. So much has the debate between deep and social ecologists biased many well-meaning people against social ecology that a certain moral pressure obliges them to call themselves "deep ecologists" and criticize "left-ism" and "social ecology" even when they actually behave as social ecologists and even when some of them clearly have leftist back-grounds. Even Judi Bari, with her long-time background as an IWW labor organizer, has denied that she is a "leftist" and has argued that no "leftist theory" has ever spoken to the need for creating an ecological society.[2] She also continues to misrepresent my views. I was shocked to read recently her unfounded assertion that I believe in anthropcentr-ism and that "human beings are a *higher* form of life."[3]

This continuing hostility to social ecology raises the question: What lies at the core of the deep ecology versus social ecology dispute? Let me start by eliminating a formidable obstacle that stands in the way of clearly understanding this dispute. I've been told by a friend that many people regard the whole dispute as personal, in fact as a form of "ego-tripping" or "ego-bashing" on my part. This is simply not the case.

I was on very good personal terms with Bill Devall and a number of other prominent deep ecologists up to 1987, despite my concerns about the implications of their views. In 1986, I even received a warm season's greeting from Devall with the remark: "Happy winter solstice! I hope we can continue our conversation and I feel I have much to learn from you." Devall and Sessions's *Deep Ecology* had nothing but praise for my book, *The Ecology of Freedom.* Up until 1987, I simply had no reason for *personal* hostility towards any prominent deep ecology thinker or activist.

It is also rather petty, I think, for deep ecologist Christopher Manes to suggest in his recent book *Green Rage* that the reason I criticized deep ecology was because I was in some sense personally envious of deep ecology's ability to "touch people's lives," while "social ecology succeeded only in sweeping the halls of the Institute for Social Ecology."[4] At seventy years of age, I have neither the energy nor the time to envy anyone about anything—much less anyone's success in the ecology movement. My own life's work is basically finished, and I am reasonably content with it.

My concern about the growing popularity of deep ecology is political not personal. In contrast to Bill Devall's contention that deep ecology is becoming a very embattled anti-establishmentarian body of ideas, I find that it has actually become very trendy and chic these days. It has not only swept into its fold a large number of well-situated academics but also a lot of journalists and even royalty, like Prince Philip of England, and other movers and shakers in the elite "ecology" establishment. My question is, have these recent converts to deep ecology become radical social critics or is deep ecology congenial to their conventional, and sometimes even reactionary, social views?

Whatever its merits, the fact is that deep ecology, more than any other "radical" ecological perspective, blames "Humanity" as such for the ecological crisis—especially ordinary "consumers" and "breeders of children"—while largely ignoring the corporate interests that are really plundering the planet. This socially neutral aspect of deep ecology appears to be very agreeable to the powers that be. I think this is the key reason that out of all the possible "radical" schools of ecological thought, deep ecology is being celebrated in popular magazines, in newspapers, on television, and in other media. When even so distinguished a writer and so socially committed a deep ecologist as Gary Snyder can write, "Mankind has become a locust-like blight on the planet," I am left to wonder what is so "radical" about deep ecology.[5] Can one join this crowd and still enjoy the luxury of calling oneself a "radical ecologist?"

Please let us keep personalities and matters of "ego" out of the discussion, then, and let us stick to the *politics* that are really involved in the dispute. No one should forget that it is a strictly political fact that the late Ed Abbey, so revered by many self-professed deep ecologists, described the "traditions and ideals" of the United States as a "product of northern European civilization" and warned us against allowing "our" country to be "Latinized."[6] It is a strictly political fact that he described Hispanic immigrants as "hungry, ignorant, unskilled, and culturally-morally-generically impoverished people."[7] It is a strictly political fact that "Miss Ann Thropy" (who, I am advised by prominent Earth First!ers, is Christopher Manes) welcomed the AIDS epidemic as "a necessary solution" to the "population problem" (generously including "war, famine, humiliating poverty" along with AIDS) and wrote: "To paraphrase Voltaire: if the AIDS epidemic didn't exist, radical environmentalists would have to invent one."[8] It is also a strictly political fact that Dave himself declared, in his now regretted *Simply*

Living interview with Bill Devall, that "the worst thing we could do in Ethiopia is to give aid—the best thing would be to just let nature seek its own balance, to let the people there just starve."[9]

I could go on almost indefinitely citing such remarks and the unhealthy moral climate they created. But I'm sure people are sick of it—certainly I am. I bring it up here again simply to remind people of the atmosphere that gave rise to my criticisms of deep ecology in 1987. This is all too often ignored. Even so respectable an academic deep ecologist as Warwick Fox persists in repeating my sharp attacks of 1987, pulling angry quotes out of my original "Social Ecology versus Deep Ecology" article without giving his readers the least hint as to the harshly misanthropic statements that inspired my anger in the first place.[10]

I'm sorry to say that this approach leaves strong doubts in my mind about the moral integrity of many of my deep ecology critics. This concern is even further heightened by the fact that after I sharply attacked these chilling statements by self-professed deep ecologists, the greater part of a year passed before the more academic deep ecologists began (often very mildly) to voice any objections to the misanthropic remarks I challenged. Even then, these objections were couched in a rather back-handed way that frequently poured abuse on me while supposedly providing critical commentary on the statements by deep ecologists that had fired my anger. Indeed, many of my deep ecology critics have, over the last few years, systematically distorted my views as "anthropocentric," painted me as an enemy of wilderness, and, as in Devall's case, even red-baited me as conspiring to lead "anarchists-leftists-marxists" in a concerted "attack" on the radical ecology movement.[11]

It probably should come as no surprise that such distortions have been widely peddled by an establishment media giant such as the *New York Times* which has misquoted me as calling the Earth First! movement fascist. (I subsequently wrote the *Times* a curt letter flatly denying this allegation and voicing my support for Dave in his effort to secure his civil rights in the face of harassment by the FBI.) What is more troubling to me, however, is how so many of my deep ecology critics have themselves pushed the absurd idea that I oppose the wilderness preservation goals of Earth First!, or that I think Earth First! activists are "eco-fascists." Dave has been one of the few deep ecologists who has engaged me in a principled and respectful manner. I have appreciated his openness and integrity.

However, the real questions that I think should concern us are these: Are the misanthropic views expressed by the more blunt and presumably extreme deep ecologists mere accidents? Do they simply emerge from purely personal proclivities, or do they have roots in deep ecology's basic ideology? Leaving aside all the storm and fury of earlier debates, these questions should be of real concern to us.

In the course of this dialogue, Dave Foreman has clearly pulled back from the precipice of the oppressive extremes that have been articulated from within the deep ecology movement. Yet if the deep ecology principle of "biocentrism" teaches that human beings are no different from lemmings in terms of their "intrinsic worth" and the moral consideration we owe them, and if human beings are viewed as being subject to "natural laws" in just the same way as any other species, then these "extreme" statements are really the *logical* conclusion of deep ecology philosophy.

Some deep ecologists such as Warwick Fox have used harsh words in condemning Dave's old views on famine in Ethiopia. Yet, if one is consistently "biocentric," one can easily come to believe that Ethiopian children should be left to starve just as any animal species that uses up its food supply will starve. And one can also easily come to believe that AIDS is "nature's revenge" for "excessive" population growth, ecological damage, and the like. According to "natural law," if lemmings' food supplies increase, their population will naturally increase to numbers that make them vulnerable to a die-off. Similarly, from a "biocentric" perspective, if there is a surplus of available food for people, human populations will automatically swell to numbers that eventually make them vulnerable to a die-off by making them so destructive of their environment until it can no longer support them.

It was on the basis of this line of thinking that Dave originally spoke of letting "nature seek its own balance," of letting "the people [in Ethiopia] just starve." If one goes no further than "biocentrism" for one's primary guide to ecological wisdom, this is presumably a "natural" point of view. It should come as no surprise then that Bill Devall didn't find anything wrong with Dave's conclusions about Ethiopian children, either while he conducted the original interview in *Simple Living* or after I so inconveniently entered the fray—or that such statements were so lightly criticized, if at all, by Arne Naess, George Sessions, or other leading exponents of deep ecology. Such attitudes are simply a logical extension of biocentrism.

But herein lies the rub: Are people really *only* biological beings? Are they subject to exactly the same fluctuations in population that we find in the animal and plant world? I certainly do not wish to deny that, in fairly localized regional economies, bad weather, pest infestations, and unsound ecological practices can result in the deaths of innumerable people. But people, far more than any other animal species of which I am aware, are intensely *cultural* beings. Having emerged out of a long process of evolutionary development in which they were often subject to so-called "natural laws" in an evolutionary phase that we can call "*first* nature," humans have created a cultural and social line of evolution of their own. This evolution is based on highly institutionalized societies that I have called "*second* nature."

Now, the existence of second nature doesn't mean that human beings are any less animal-like or "natural" than lemmings. But *added* to their primate bodies and possibly inborn communal tendencies is a highly complex cultural nexus of economic relations, symbolic forms of communication, hierarchies, classes, systems of domination and exploitation, political institutions, cities, technologies, and gender roles that greatly determine their population growth and overall environmental impact.

Terrible as I believe a great deal of human history has been, we cannot ignore the overwhelming fact that the human species—itself a product of natural evolution—is no longer simply subject to "natural laws." Human beings can play an appallingly destructive role for non-human life-forms, or by the same token, they can play a profoundly constructive role. This is not preordained by "natural law." Similarly, people can have an appallingly destructive or a profoundly constructive impact upon their own economic relations, forms of communication, political institutions, cities, and technologies. They can create an ecological society, or they can easily destroy their own tenure on the planet.

This superadded "cultural" ensemble markedly distinguishes human beings from all animals in terms of their lifeways and their impact on the natural world. For example, unlike lemmings, human beings can redistribute their food supplies or they can accumulate their resources for a privileged few while denying them to the oppressed many. They can also establish codes of sexual behavior that determine population growth rates or change the social conditions that prompt people to have many children. Like it or not, this entirely new line of social evolution—second nature—has had a vast, all-encompassing effect upon all biological evolution, including first nature itself.

Since this is true, we cannot simply wish away human social development as such by evoking images of a "return" to the wild Pleistocene or the benign Neolithic. Rather, we must honestly ask ourselves: How can human social development be brought into the ecology picture? Must we separate our ecological problems from our social problems? Must we regard human population fluctuations as merely matters of "natural law?" Must we ignore human suffering and thereby unconsciously blunt our sensitivity to suffering in the non-human world?

I do not claim that all deep ecologists hold the views I have laid out here, of course. Dave has certainly modified some of his views in very significant ways. Indeed, a few deep ecologists even tell us that they are no less socially conscious than social ecologists. Yet this is rare, and when you ask them how their social consciousness relates to ecological issues, they usually become vague at best. It seems to be one of the most unfortunate features of deep ecology that its academic acolytes, knowing so very little about social theory (despite the fact that many of them are academic sociologists), have created a notion of "biocentricity" in which human social development plays a secondary role, if any, to natural development; in which population growth is treated exclusively as though it were a biological issue; and in which non-human suffering is placed on a par with human suffering in almost purely zoological terms.

Given that I believe that "biocentrism" is flawed at its conceptual roots, my deep ecology critics usually regard me as "anthropocentric." But my point is not to denigrate the struggle to save and even increase wild areas, or the struggle to save forests from the lumber companies and developers, or the struggle to preserve and extend the range of wildlife and promote natural diversity. I have spoken up for such positions for years. Indeed, it is a shameful slander to even suggest that I do not support the struggles of Earth First! and its militants.

Thus, to those who dismiss me as "anthropocentric," I must ask: Why must I be forced to choose between "biocentrism" and "anthropocentrism?" I never believed that the Earth was "made" for human exploitation. In fact, as a dyed-in-the-wool secularist, I never believed it was "made" at all. I also don't believe that humans should "dominate" nature—the ultimate impossibility of this is a key idea in social ecology. Given my longstanding fascination with the wonders of natural evolution and, yes, wilderness, what need do I have for a "biocentrism" that deflects me from the social roots of the ecological crisis? I believe that non-human and human nature are as inextricably bound to each other as the ventricles of the heart are bound to the auricles and that both human and non-human nature deserve moral consideration. An "anthropocentrism" that is based on the religious principle that the Earth was "made" to be dominated by "Humanity" is as remote from my thinking as a "biocentrism" that turns human society into just another community of animals. We need a much better perspective, I think. Whether there will be any wild areas or wildlife left in a century or so depends decisively upon the kind of society we will have—not on whether we lecture the human species over its failings, call it a "cancer" or worse on the planet, or extol the virtues of the Pleistocene or Neolithic. It will depend not only on our attitude toward non-human life but on the extent to which countless social oppressions are permitted to exist that compel peasants to cut down forests in order to survive, and that destroy their traditional lifeways in the bargain.

Even more fundamentally—and we had better get down to fundamentals if we wish to be "radical" in the real meaning of the word—whether there will be wild areas or wildlife left in a century or so depends upon whether we continue to preserve the "grow-or-die" economy (be it free-market corporate capitalism or bureaucratic state capitalism) in which an enterprise or a country that doesn't grow economically is devoured by its rivals in the domestic market or in the international arena. Indeed, until humanity can actualize its evolutionary potentialities as highly creative and ecologically-oriented beings, the antagonisms engendered by social oppression in all its forms will literally tear down the planet—both for human and for non-human life-forms alike.

To blame technology *per se* for this terrible distortion of second nature; to deal with human population growth as if it were not influenced profoundly by *cultural* factors; to reduce the basic social factors that have produced the present ecological crisis to largely, often purely *biological* ones—all this is to deflect attention away from the fact that our ecological dislocations have their primary source in *social* dislocations. The very notion of "dominating nature" has its roots in the domination of human by human—in hierarchies that brought the young into subjugation to gerontocracies, that brought women into subjugation to patriarchies, ordinary people into subjugation to military chiefdoms, working people into subjugation to capitalist or bureaucratic systems of exploitation, and so forth..

Granted, we need profound cultural changes and a new sensibility that will teach us to respect non-human life-forms; that will create new values in the production and consumption of goods; that will give rise to new life-fostering technologies rather than destructive ones; that will remove conflicts between human populations and the non-human world; and that will abet natural diversity and evolutionary development. I have written on these needs for scores of pages in books and articles. But does anyone seriously think these cultural changes can be achieved in a society that pits people against one another as buyers and sellers, as exploited and exploiters, as subjugated and subjugators at all levels of life?

To deflect our attention from these crucial social questions with a "biocentrism" that basically ignores them at best or that blames a vague "Humanity" for problems generated by a rotten social system at worst is to lead the ecology movement onto an ideological sidetrack. We have no need for "biocentrism," "anthropocentrism," or for that matter any "centrism," nor for any ideology that diverts popular attention from the social sources of the ecological crisis.

At the risk of being repetitive, let me stress that deep ecology's limited, and sometimes distorted, social understanding explains why no other "radical" ecology philosophy could be more congenial to the ruling elites of our time. Here is a perspective on the ecological crisis that blames our "values" without going to the social sources of these values. It denounces population growth without explaining why the poor and oppressed proliferate in such huge numbers or what social changes could humanely stabilize the human population. It blames technology without asking who develops it and for what purposes. It denounces consumers without dealing with the grow-or-die economy that uses its vast media apparatus to get them to consume as a monstrous substitute for a culturally and spiritually meaningful life.

To fail to explore these issues, give coherent explanations of them, or provide a clear sense of direction in dealing with them, is to completely bypass the core problems that confront ecologically-minded people today. It amounts to separating the ecology movement from the struggles of women for complete gender equality, people of color for racial equality, the poor for economic equality, subcultures like gays and lesbians for social equality, the oppressed of all kinds for human equality. Characteristically, the literature produced by most deep ecologists takes little—if any—note of lead poisoning in ghettos. It rarely, if ever, deals with workplace pollution, and the special environmental hazards that face women, ethnic minorities, and city dwellers. Laudable as Earth First!'s reverence for wild areas and wildlife may be, the failure of deep ecology to provide a radical social orientation to its admirers often leaves them as mere acolytes of a wilderness cult. Further, in its totally misplaced attack on "Humanity" deep ecology alienates many sympathetic activists who may respect wild areas and wildlife as much as deep ecologists do, but who are unwilling to flirt with misanthropy and self-hatred.

Limits of space do not permit me to cite all my reasons for regarding deep ecology as far from "deep." What I must stress is that social ecology is neither "biocentric" nor "anthropocentric." Rather, it is *naturalistic*. Because of this naturalist orientation, social ecology is no less concerned with issues like the integrity of wild areas and wildlife than are "biocentrists." As a hiker, an ecologist, and above all a naturalist who devoutly believes in freedom, I can talk as passionately as any deep ecologist about the trails I have followed, the vistas I have gazed at, or the soaring hawks I have watched for hours from cliffs and mountain peaks. Yet social ecology is also naturalistic in the very important sense that it stresses humanity's and society's profound roots in natural evolution. Hence my use of the term "second *nature*" to emphasize the development of human social life out of the natural world.

This second aspect of social ecology's naturalistic perspective not only challenges misanthropy; it challenges conventional social theory as well. The philosophy of social ecology denies that there can be a complete separation—let alone a desirable opposition—between human and non-human evolution. As naturalists, we respect the fact that human beings have evolved out of first or non-human nature as mammals and primates to form a new domain composed of mutable institutions, technologies, values, forms of communication. Social ecology recognizes that we are both biological *and* social beings. Indeed, social ecologists go so far as to carefully analyze the important social history that has pitted humanity not only against itself but, very significantly, against non-human nature as well.

Over the centuries, as I have said many times before, social conflicts have fostered the development of hierarchies and classes based on domination and exploitation in which the great majority of human beings have been as ruthlessly exploited as the natural world itself. Social ecology carefully focuses on this social history and reveals that the very *idea* of dominating nature stems from the domination of human by human. This hierarchical mentality and system has been extended out from the social domination of people—particularly the young, women, people of color, and yes, males generally as workers and subjects—into the realm of non-human nature. Thus, unlike most deep ecologists, social ecologists understand that until we undertake the project of liberating human beings from domination and hierarchy—not only economic exploitation and class rule, as orthodox socialists would have it—our chances of saving the wild areas of the planet and wildlife are remote at best.

This means that the radical ecology movement must have programs for removing the oppressions that people suffer even while some of us are primarily focused on the damage this society is inflicting on wild areas and wildlife. We should never lose sight of the fact that the project of human liberation has now become an ecological project, just as, conversely, the project of defending the Earth has also become a social project. Social ecology as a form of eco-anarchism weaves these two projects together, first by means of an organic way of thinking that I call *dialectical naturalism;* second, by means of a mutualistic social and ecological ethics that I call the *ethics of complementarity;* third, by means of a new technics that I call *eco-technology;* and last, by means of new forms of human association that I call *eco-communities.* It is not accidental that I have written works on cities as well as ecology, on utopias as well as pollution, on a new politics as well as new technologies; on a new ecological sensibility as well as a new economy. A coherent ecological philosophy must address all of these questions.

Unfortunately, many grassroots ecology activists today can not see any difference between eco-anarchism and the oppressive, industrial nightmares of Stalinism or between naturalism and "anthropocentrism." They are thus cut off from the vital and important insights that can be gleaned from the ecologically-oriented, left libertarian tradition. Even Judi Bari, with her leftist background, seems to have trouble making such important distinctions. In an open letter to Dave after his resignation from Earth First!, she argued that Earth First! had no connection to the left, saying, "We are too irreverent and we have too much of a sense of humor to be considered leftists."[12] I must remind Bari, however, of the simple fact that humor and playfulness have been integral parts of the libertarian left for generations.

Not all leftists are poker-faced Stalinists, Maoists, or unimaginative liberal reformers. Wasn't it the Industrial Workers of the World (IWW), the largely anarcho-syndicalist "Wobblies," who prepared one of the most hilarious songbooks in labor history, whose shenanigans drove the union-busters mad with fury—and whose pranks form the haunting, if largely unconscious, inspiration of Earth First! itself? Wasn't it the anarchic New Left of Paris in May-June 1968 that painted the city with such marvelous slogans as "Imagination To Power!" "Be Realistic! Demand The Impossible!" and "I Take My Desires To Be Reality Because I Believe In The Reality Of My Desires?" Wasn't it the anarchist Emma Goldman, after all, who said that she didn't want to be in any revolution in which she couldn't dance?

In closing, I just want to repeat that the ongoing debate and dialogue is not a matter of personalities, at least not so far as I'm concerned; it is a matter of very real political concerns about where the ecology movement is heading. Much as I love wild areas and wildlife, much as I recall the magnificent vistas and the quiet sense of freedom I've always felt in our forests, I will not ignore the social causes and the human suffering that lie at the roots of our ecological crisis and the absence of an ecological sensibility. I will not stand up as a judgmental pundit in an academic ivory tower or as a misanthropic wilderness activist and preach against a despicable "Humanity" while lecturing to it about the glories of a vague abstraction called "Nature."

Nature is very real and concrete to me, a living, ever-changing and wondrous development—as are its very real products called human beings. I refuse to mystify either "nature" or "humanity" at the expense of the other in the name of a simplistic, one-sided pair of ethical alternatives called "biocentrism" and "anthropocentrism." I reject the need to make a choice between such abstractions with so little validity. I claim the right to be a naturalist *and* a leftist who rises above both vague simplifications and who relates the problems of ecological dislocations to those of social dislocations in the name of a social ecology.

One of my major goals is to foster the development of a non-hierarchical ethics of complementarity among humans *and* between humanity and non-human life. This should be the fundamental starting point, the unshakable common ground, of the radical ecology movement. Perhaps the greatest contribution of this dialogue between Dave Foreman and myself is that it proves if radical ecologists can agree on this as their common ground, we can work together and—regardless of our other disagreements—productively learn from each other. In this, I believe, lies the hope of the ecology movement.

Notes

Whither the Radical Ecology Movement?

1. Donald Worster, *Nature's Economy: A History of Ecological Ideas* (New York: Cambridge University Press, 1977), xi.

2. Andrew Dobson, *Green Political Thought* (London: Unwin Hyman, 1990), 13.

3. Murray Bookchin, *Our Synthetic Environment* (New York: Colophon, 1974), xv.

4. Arne Naess, "The Shallow and the Deep, Long-Range Ecology Movement: A Summary," *Inquiry,* No. 16, 1973, 95-100.

5. Murray Bookchin, "Crisis in the Ecology Movement," *Z Magazine,* July-August 1988, 121.

6. Warwick Fox, *Towards a Transpersonal Ecology* (Boston: Shambhala, 1990), 75.

7. Roderick Nash, *The Rights of Nature: A History of Environmental Ethics* (Madison: University of Wisconsin Press, 1989), 164-65.

8. Michael Tobias, ed., *Deep Ecology* (San Marcos: Avant Books, 1984); Bill Devall and George Sessions, *Deep Ecology: Living as if Nature Mattered* (Salt Lake City: Peregrine Smith Books, 1985).

9. Christopher Manes, *Green Rage: Radical Environmentalism and the Unmaking of Civilization* (Boston: Little, Brown & Company, 1990), 154.

10. Murray Bookchin, *Social Ecology versus Deep Ecology* (Burlington: Green Program Project, 1988), 4.

11. Edward Abbey, "U.N.C.L.E.," *Utne Reader,* March-April 1988, 7.

12. Bill Devall, *Simple in Means, Rich in Ends: Practicing Deep Ecology* (Salt Lake City: Peregrine Smith Books, 1988), 136.

13. Christopher Manes, 160.

14. Roderick Nash, *Wilderness and the American Mind* (New Haven: Yale University Press, 1982), 379-388.

15. Ibid., 380.

16. Murray Bookchin, *Our Synthetic Environment,* xiv.

17. Murray Bookchin, *Remaking Society: Pathways to a Green Future* (Boston: South End Press, 1990), 155.

18. Judi Bari, "Expand Earth First!," *Earth First!,* September 22, 1990, 5.

19. René Dubos, *The Wooing of Earth* (London: Athlone Press, 1980), 1.

20. See, for example, Robyn Eckersley, "Divining Evolution: The Ecological Ethics of Murray Bookchin," *Environmental Ethics,* No. 11, 1989, 99-116. For Bookchin's challenge to this characterization of his views, see Murray Bookchin, "Recovering Evolution: A Reply to Eckersley and Fox," *Environmental Ethics,* No. 12, 1990, 253-274.

21. Murray Bookchin, *The Ecology of Freedom* (Palo Alto: Cheshire Books, 1982), 24.

22. Murray Bookchin, *Toward an Ecological Society,* (Montréal: Black Rose, 1984), 44.

23. Ibid., 59.

24. Ibid., 59.

25. John Clark ed., *Renewing the Earth: The Promise of Social Ecology* (London: Green Print, 1990), 7. For an expanded treatment of Clark's approach to environmental ethics, see his essay "Ecology, Technology, and Respect for Nature" in John Clark, *The Anarchist Moment: Reflections on Culture, Nature, and Power* (Montréal: Black Rose, 1984), 191-199.

26. Thomas Berry, "The World of René Dubos," *Amicus Journal* Winter 1991, 52.

27. For a critical examination of one social ecologist's anthropocentric environmental ethic, see Steve Chase, "Beyond Sustainability: What Green Activists Can and Can't Learn From C. George Benello," in Julian Benello *et. al.* eds., *From the Ground Up: Essays on Grassroots and Workplace Democracy* (Boston: South End Press, forthcoming).

28. René Dubos, *So Human an Animal* (New York: Scribners, 1968), 206.

29. René Dubos, *The Wooing of Earth,* 134.

30. John Clark ed., *Renewing the Earth,* 5.

31. Ibid. This oversight on the part of a 1990 anthology which attempts to show how the philosophy of social ecology expresses "in a comprehensive, richly developed, and profound manner the deepest strivings of the Green Movement" is quite glaring.

32. Quoted in Christopher Manes, 66.

33. Quoted in Ibid., 225.

34. Quoted in Rik Scarce, *Eco-Warriors: Understanding the Radical Environmental Movement* (Chicago: Noble Press, 1990), 66.

35. Christopher Manes, 74.

36. Arne Naess, *Ecology, Community and Lifestyle* (New York: Cambridge University Press, 1989), 29.

37. Shepard's influence is very strong in Bill Devall and George Sessions, *Deep Ecology,* particularly in their chapter "Culture and Character," 179-191. For those who want to go straight to the source, see Paul Shepard, *Thinking*

Animals: Animals and the Development of Human Intelligence (New York: Viking, 1978); and Paul Shepard, *Nature and Madness* (San Francisco: Sierra Club Books, 1982).

38. Quoted in Roderick Nash, *Wilderness and the American Mind*, 253.

39. Quoted in Ibid., 252.

40. Dave Foreman, "Whither Earth First!," *Earth First* November 1, 1987, 21.

41. Murray Bookchin, *Remaking Society*, 153.

42. Quoted in Christopher Manes, 84.

43. Edward Abbey, *One Life At A Time, Please* (New York: Henry Holt, 1988), 43.

44. Marti Kheel, "Ecofemnism and Deep Ecology" in Irene Diamond and Gloria Feman Orenstein, eds., *Reweaving the World: The Emergence of Ecofeminism* (San Francisco: Sierra Club Books, 1990) 128-154; Ynestra King, "Coming of Age with the Greens," *Z Magazine*, February 1988, 18-19; Janet Biehl, "It's Deep, But Is It Broad? An Eco-Feminist Looks at Deep Ecology," *Kick It Over,* (Special supplement, date unknown); Carl Anthony, "Why Blacks Should be Environmentalists," in Brad Erickson, ed., *Call to Action: A Handbook for Ecology, Peace and Justice* (San Francisco: Sierra Club Books, 1990), 144-145; Dana Alston, ed., *We Speak For Ourselves: Social Justice, Race and Environment* (Washington: Panos Institute, 1991).

45. Dave Foreman, "Reinhabitation, Biocentrism and Self Defense," *Earth First!,* August 1, 1987, 22.

46. Dave Foreman, *Ecodefense: A Field Guide to Monkeywrenching* (Tucson: Ned Ludd Books, 1989), 16.

47. Dave Foreman Interview by Bill Devall, in *Simple Living,* Vol. 2, No. 12, 1986.

48. Murray Bookchin, *Remaking Society*, 46.

49. Bill Devall, *Simple in Means, Rich in Ends,* 137.

50. "Principles of the Left Green Network" adopted at the first Conference of the Left Green Network, Ames, Iowa, April 21-23, 1989.

51. Earth Action Network newsletter, October 1990.

Looking for Common Ground

1. Roderick Nash, *The Rights of Nature: A History of Environmental Ethics,* 164.

2. Warwick Fox, "The Deep Ecology-Ecofeminism Debate and its Parallels," *Environmental Ethics,* No. 11, 1989, n38.

3. Arne Naess, "Finding Common Ground," *Green Synthesis,* No. 30, March 1989, 9.

4. Raymond Dasmann works with bioregionalist Peter Berg at the Planet Drum Foundation which publishes the *Raise the Stakes* newspaper and been helped organize the North American bioregional movement.

5. For a look at Foreman's initial position on immigration, see Dave Foreman, "Is Sanctuary the Answer?," *Earth First,* November 1, 1987, 21-22.

6. For a full presentation of Ehrenfeld's critical view of humanism, see David Ehrenfeld, *The Arrogance of Humanism* (New York: Oxford University Press, 1978).

7. For a full presentation of Simon's critical view of ecological limit to growth theories, see Julian Simon, *The Ultimate Resource,* (Princeton: Princeton University Press, 1981).

Ecology and the Left

1. Arne Naess, *Ecology, Community and Lifestyle,* 29.

2. For a full discussion of the Spanish Anarchist movement see, Murray Bookchin, *The Spanish Anarchists: The Heroic Years, 1868-1936* (New York: Harper Colophon, 1977); Sam Dolgoff, ed., *The Anarchist Collectives* (New York: Free Life Editions, 1974).

3. Karl Marx, *Grundrisse* (New York: Random House, 1973), 410. For a full discussion of Bookchin's critique of Marx's nature philosophy, see "Marxism as Bourgeois Sociology" in Murray Bookchin, *Toward an Ecological Society,* 195-210.

Radical Visions and Strategies

1. For a full presentation of Foreman's vision of Big Wilderness, see "Dreaming Big Wilderness" in Dave Foreman, *Confessions of an Eco-Warrior* (New York: Harmony Books, 1991), 177-192.

2. Murray Bookchin, "The New Municipal Agenda" in *The Rise of Urbanization and the Decline of Citizenship* (San Francisco: Sierra Club Books, 1987), 225-288; Murray Bookchin, "Theses on Libertarian Municipalism" in *The Limits of the City* (Montréal: Black Rose, 1980), 164-184.

Racism and the Future of the Movement

1. For more information about the movement for environmental justice, see Robert Bullard, *Dumping in Dixie: Race, Class and Environmental Quality* (Boulder: Westview Press, 1990); Dana Alston, ed., *We Speak For Ourselves: Social Justice, Race and Environment.*

2. Henry David Thoreau, "Civil Disobedience" in *The Portable Thoreau* (New York: Penguin Books, 1975), 120.

Second Thoughts of an Eco-Warrior

1. Dave Foreman Interview by Bill Devall in *Simple Living.*

2. For a good history of the COINTELPRO program, see Ward Churchill and Jim Vander Wall, *The COINTELPRO Papers: Documents from the FBI's Secret Wars Against Dissent in the United States* (Boston, South End Press, 1990); for a good activist's guide to protecting your movement from such tactics, see Brian Glick, *War at Home: Covert Action Against U.S. Activists and What We Can Do About It* (Boston: South End Press, 1989).

3. William Ophuls, *Ecology and the Politics of Scarcity* (San Francisco: W.H. Freeman, 1977), 9.

4. William Catton, Jr., *Overshoot: The Ecological Basis of Revolutionary Change* (Urbana: University of Illinois Press, 1980), 126.

5. Aldo Leopold, *A Sand County Almanac* (New York: Oxford University Press, 1949), 202.

6. Ibid., 224-225.

7. For a full presentation of Taylor's interpretation of the "biocentric outlook," see Paul Taylor, *Respect for Nature: A Theory of Environmental Ethics* (Princeton: Princeton University Press, 1986).

8. Arne Naess, "Finding Common Ground," 9.

9. "Principles of Social Ecology" from the Institute for Social Ecology's 1991 Summer Program catalogue.

Where I Stand Now

1. Judi Bari, "Expand Earth First!," 5.

2. Ibid.

3. Judi Bari, "Why I am not a Misanthrope," *Earth First!,* February 2, 1991, 25.

4. Christopher Manes, 156.

5. Quoted in Bill Devall and George Sessions, *Deep Ecology,* 171.

6. Edward Abbey, "Letter to the Editor," *Bloomsbury Review,* April-May 1986.

7. Edward Abbey, *One Life At A Time, Please,* 43.

8. Miss Ann Thropy (pseud.), "Population and AIDS," *Earth First!,* May 1, 1987, 32.

9. Dave Foreman Interview by Bill Devall in *Simple Living.*

10. For an example of Fox's treatment of Bookchin's criticisms of deep ecology, see Warwick Fox, *Towards a Transpersonal Ecology,* 49.

11. Bill Devall, "Deep Ecology and Its Critics," *Earth First!,* December 22, 1987, 18.

12. Judi Bari, "Expand Earth First!," 5.

Index

of social hierarchy in thought of,
22, 129, 131; on spirituality, 33,
34-36; on strategic views of, 81-
85; on support for Earth First!,
36; on wilderness preservation,
14, 127
Bryant, Bunyon, 94
Buckley, William, 48
Burlington Greens, 23, 27
Bush, George, 42

C

Carrying capacity, 29, 79, 113-15
Carson, Rachel, 28
Carter, Jimmy, 37, 66
Catton, William, 115
Capitalism, 57, 72; ecological degra-
dation and, 31, 88
Chodorkoff, Dan, 28
CIA, 42, 108
Civil Rights Movement, 27
Clamshell Alliance, 27
Clark, John, 15, 16
Class consciousness, 51
COINTELPPO, 112
Colorado River, 67
Communism, 54-55
Community economics, 81
Community organizing, 82, 99-102
Complementarity. *See* ethics of
complementarity
Confederation, 83, 84-85
Congress of Racial Equality, 98
Conservation biology, 117
Conservation movement, 49; Earth
First! criticisms of, 16-17; lim-
ited reformism of, 67-69, 71-72
Constructive criticism in alliance
building, 92-93
Co-optation, 71, 76-79
Counterculture, 27
Counter-Enlightenment. *See* En-
lightenment ideals

D

Dasman, Raymond, 40
Davidoff, Linda, on reformism, 63-
65, 99, 121
Decentralization, energy sources
and production, 80; objections
to, 85; urban and rural, 79
Deep Ecology (Sessions and
Devall), 10, 107, 122
Deep ecology, basic principles of,
18, 53; Bookchin's contribution
to, 9-10; Earth First! and, 10;
feminist and anti-racist critiques
of, 20, 97; Foreman's influence
in, 9; generic meaning, 8; key
thinkers in, 9; Kropotkin's influence in, 13; left libertarian ideas
in, 61-62; limited social theory
of, 19-21, 96-97, 127, 129-30;
misanthropic perspectives
within, 20; perspective on overpopulation, 29-30; racism in, 95;
specific meaning, 9; tendencies
within, 117-18; value of wilderness to humans in, 18
Deep vs. social ecology, basis for
cooperation, 133; complementary differences, 36-37, 74; differing visions, 12; integrated
visions of, 23-24; journals covering debate, 10; nature of debate,
9-10, 122-23, 132; potential synthesis, 117-19; relative merits of,
62; rhetorical counter charges,
11; similar views, 96
Deloria, Jr., Vine, 115
Devall, Bill, 9, 10, 60, 61; on Bookchin, 11, 122, 124; on leftist theory, 23
Dialectical naturalism, 131
Diderot, 59
Dine (Navajo), 92
Dinosaur National Monument, 67
Dobson, Andrew, 7

WOMEN AND COUNTER-POWER

edited by Yolande Cohen

...these scholarly essays document women's political activity in antiestablishment movements, both historical and recent, in some of the nations peripheral to the powerful Western democracies and the USSR: Spain, Italy, Canada, Argentina, Algeria, Portugal, and Poland...The authors'...material provides information, as well as insights, not readily available elsewhere.

Small Press

Each author presents not only the historical importance of the women's struggle, but also its contradictions and ambivalence.

Espace, Population et Societe

244 pages
Paperback ISBN: 0-921689-10-1   **$19.95**
Hardcover ISBN: 0-921689-11-X   **$39.95**
Women/Politics/History

GERMANY EAST

Dissent and Opposition 2nd revised edition

by Bruce Allen

[a] very well researched and comprehensive backgrounder.
Books in Canada
...well written...designed to inform and encourage solidarity
Choice
...a refreshing glimpse into life beyond the rusting iron curtain.
Peace Magazine
...a useful brief survey of dissent in East Germany.
Small Press

This revised edition brings up to date the drama that took place with the coming down of the Berlin Wall and the re-unification of Germany.

191 pages
Paperback ISBN: 0-921689-96-9   **$16.95**
Hardcover ISBN: 0-921689-97-7   **$35.95**
Politics/History

THE ANARCHIST COLLECTIVES
Workers' Self-Management in Spain 1936-39
edited by Sam Dolgoff

Sam Dolgoff, editor of the best anthology of Bakunin's writings, has now produced an excellent documentary history of the anarchist collectives in Spain. Although there is a vast literature on the Spanish Civil War, this is the first book in English that is devoted to the experiments in workers' self-management, both urban and rural, which constituted one of the most remarkable social revolutions in modern history.
Paul Avrich

The eyewitness reports and commentary presented in this highly important study reveal a very different understanding of the nature of socialism and the means for achieving it.
Noam Chomsky

195 pages, illustrated
Paperback ISBN: 0-919618-74-X $14.95
Hardcover ISBN: 0-919618-73-1 $29.95
History/Politics/Philosophy

DURRUTI
The People Armed
by Abel Paz
translated by Nancy MacDonald

An exhaustive biography of the legendary Spanish revolutionary Buenaventura Durruti, who died at age forty in 1936. Durruti was an uncompromising anarchist who knew battle, exile, imprisonment, strikes, insurrections, and life underground. This man, who started life as a rebellious young worker and who at his death was mourned by millions, acted always on the conviction that freedom and revolution are inseparable, refusing all honours, awards and bureaucratic positions.

Wherever you go it's Durruti and Durruti again, whom you hear spoken of as a wonder man.
Toronto Daily star

323 pages, illustrated
Paperback ISBN: 0-919618-74-X $14.95
Hardcover ISBN: 0-919618-73-1 $29.95
Biography/History/Politics

WHEN FREEDOM WAS LOST
The Unemployed, The Agitator, and the State
by Lorne Brown

An examination of an important chapter in Canadian history, the 1930's, when thousands of unemployed men were forced into work camps and subjected to poor living conditions, slave wages, and military discipline. Brown's factual and moving history records the desperation, disillusionment, and rebellion of these welfare inmates, and the repressive and shameful way in which the politicians and government authorities tried to keep the situation under control.

Lorne Brown seeks to remedy the dearth of the 30's labour Canadiana with this study of little-known labour camps.
Books In Canada

208 pages, photographs
Paperback ISBN: 0-920057-77-2   **$14.95**
Hardcover ISBN: 0-920057-75-6   **$36.95**
History/Labour/Politics

THE SEARCH FOR COMMUNITY
From Utopia to a Co-operative Society
by George Melnyk

Co-ops in capitalist and communist nations alike are assessed for strengths and drawbacks — whether religious, nationalist, cultural, social or economic in basis. Using his extensive knowledge of developments on the international scene, Melnyk selects the components that can be adapted to our society and used to link groups already functioning. The result is the *social co-operative*, a new citizen-run structure that will successfully respond to our social and economic requirements.

Melnyk offers a fascinating social history of co-operatives, from monastery to commune.
Choice

170 pages
Paperback ISBN: 0-920057-52-7   **$16.95**
Hardcover ISBN: 0-920057-53-5   **$36.95**
Sociology/History/Politics

TURNING THE TIDE

The U.S. and Latin America
2nd revised edition
by Noam Chomsky

Regarding U.S. policy in Latin America, *Turning The Tide* succinctly provides the most cogent available descriptions of what is going on, and why. It will be a central tool for everyone who wants to promote peace and justice in the Americas.

Noam Chomsky reveals the aim and impact of U.S. policy in Latin America by examining the historical record and current events. With this as a backdrop, he also shows the connection between Latin American policy and broader nuclear international politics and explains the logic and role of the Cold War for both the super powers. Finally, Chomsky looks at why we accept Reaganesque rhetoric in the light of the role of the media and the intelligentsia in the numbing of our awareness. He concludes by describing what we can do to resist.

The degree to which Mr. Chomsky can not only challenge, but also persuasively reverse claims about those forces responsible for the worst repression and aggression in Central America should jolt any fair-minded person who still buys the Administration's moral case for current US policy.
New York Times

Noam Chomsky is professor of linguistics and philosophy, and Institute Professor at M.I.T. He has been the recipient of honorary degrees from the University of London, University of Chicago, Delhi University, and four other colleges and universities. He is fellow of the American Academy of Arts and Sciences, member of the National Academy of Arts and Sciences, and member of the National Academy of Sciences, and author of numerous books and articles on linguistics, philosophy, intellectual history and contemporary issues.

300 pages
Paperback ISBN: 0-920057-91-8　　　　　**$16.95**
Hardcover ISBN: 0-920057-90-X　　　　　**$36.95**
International Politics